FORTUNE OF WOLVES

ALSO BY RYAN GRIFFITH

Lutz

FORTUNE
OF
WOLVES

RYAN GRIFFITH

PLAYWRIGHTS CANADA PRESS
TORONTO

LIBRARY AND ARCHIVES CANADA CATALOGUING IN PUBLICATION
Title: Fortune of wolves / Ryan Griffith.
Names: Griffith, Ryan, author.
Description: A play.
Identifiers: Canadiana (print) 20190186712 | Canadiana (ebook) 20190186747 | ISBN 9780369100351 (softcover) | ISBN 9780369100368 (PDF) | ISBN 9780369100375 (EPUB) | ISBN 9780369100382 (Kindle)
Classification: LCC PS8613.R557 F67 2019 | DDC C812/.6—dc23

Playwrights Canada Press acknowledges that we operate on land, which, for thousands of years, has been the traditional territories of the Mississaugas of the Credit, Huron-Wendat, Anishinaabe, Métis, and Haudenosaunee peoples. Today, this meeting place is home to many Indigenous peoples from across Turtle Island, and we are grateful to have the opportunity to work and play here.

We acknowledge the financial support of the Canada Council for the Arts—which last year invested $153 million to bring the arts to Canadians throughout the country—the Ontario Arts Council (OAC), Ontario Creates, and the Government of Canada for our publishing activities.

 Canada Council for the Arts Conseil des arts du Canada

 ONTARIO ARTS COUNCIL CONSEIL DES ARTS DE L'ONTARIO an Ontario government agency un organisme du gouvernement de l'Ontario

Canada  ONTARIO CREATES | ONTARIO CRÉATIF

For you, lone wolf.

PERFORMANCE RULES

1. Play with a six-sided die, or any spinning-wheel-equivalent device with only six outcomes.

2. No performance of the play should exceed thirty-six monologues.

3. All monologues by Lowell must be performed.

4. The following monologues are also recommended as "mandatory":

   September #6
   November #6
   December #1
   January #2 and #5
   March #2, #3, or #4, and #6
   June (II) #1 and #2

5. The remaining monologues may be included/excluded on a nightly basis, refreshed by rolling the dice.

6. Any or all rules may be thoughtfully discarded as the play's director/company sees fit.

Fortune of Wolves was first produced by Theatre New Brunswick at Open Space Theatre in Fredericton, New Brunswick, from October 12 to 30, 2017, before touring the province. It featured the following cast and creative team:

Carlos Gonzalez-Vio
Kimwun Perehinec
Michaela Washburn
Graham Percy

Director: Thomas Morgan Jones
Sound Designer/Composer: Deanna Choi
Lighting Designer: David DeGrow
Costume Designer: Sherry Kinnear
Stage Manager: Tammy Faulkner
Assistant Director: Victoria Stacey
Carpentry: Jamie Atkinson
Props/Scenic Painting: Elaine Bellefontaine
Props/Paint Assistant: Billy Doucet

CHIEF ARCHIVIST'S NOTE

The interviews contained in this archive were transcribed by Lt. Amit Khanna shortly after a box of audio cassettes and journals were recovered from the ruins of an A-frame structure in quadrant **cf7893-2** of the North Central Wastelands in late **August 42 P.D.**

Data recovery proved difficult. Despite careful storage and processing, the tapes disintegrated rapidly. As a result, Lt. Khanna's early transcripts are all that remain of the source materials. The journals contained fragmented stories, as well as some crude notes regarding the ages, names, and locations of the interview subjects from the tapes.

This archive is classified and restricted to personnel below **level 7** clearance. Penalties for personnel accessing archived materials above their clearance level include dismemberment and/or death, in accordance with **section 73** of the **New Union Settlement Information Security Act (X.C.73)**.

Silentium in umbra,
Col. Grace Edmonds

Settlement 21
23/10/52 P.D.

JUNE

LOWELL (DARTMOUTH, NS)

I come from big noise.

My parents bought a house near the beach in Lawrencetown. Nova Scotia. That's where we lived for years—Mom and Dad and me.

The house was close enough that we could hear the waves crashing on the shore. I would lie on my bed with the bedroom window open at night and just listen to the surf roll in. It's a very full sound. Full of water and force and gravity and life and impact and action and movement and nature . . . full of everything. Full of stuff we know and stuff we don't know. Cosmic and juggernaut, rhythmic and natural. Growing up, I got used to sound like this. Constant music. Big noise.

Dad bought me some recording equipment for my fourteenth birthday. So I'd head down to the beach and just let the tapes . . . catch everything. I didn't just record the beach, though. I'd record my friends talking sometimes. When we hung out . . . Connor, JP, and Jane. I'd get Dad to take me into Halifax some weekends when he was working, and I would walk around the city with the recorder on.

I used to hide the recorder in different parts of our house and leave it running. Sometimes it would catch parts of conversations my parents were having. The arguments they had. Or Mom talking on the phone. Dad snoring on the couch with the television still on.

My parents died in a car accident. A few years ago now. A deer jumped out in front of them. Dad swerved. The car went off the road. It flipped upside down and landed in the cove. They weren't able to get out, so they drowned.

A lot of car accidents happen when people are almost home. It's just a weird fact. The little cove my parents drowned in—you could see it from my bedroom window.

But, right now, I'm sitting on the kitchen floor in my grandmother's apartment on Ochterloney Street. In Dartmouth. Which
isn't Lawrencetown, but it's still in Nova Scotia. Right across the
water from Halifax. It's part of Halifax, but it's basically the dark
side of Halifax. That's where I'm recording this.

My grandmother . . . she spent her entire life in Dartmouth.
Never married, but she had a kid . . . my dad, and she raised him
alone. Then my dad moved out of her house and met my mom when
he started going to university. He was studying medicine. Anyway,
so my mom, she got pregnant, and they had me. We lived out near
Lawrencetown . . . but I already talked about all of that. When my
parents died, I ended up moving in with my grandmother, and it
was just me and her. We looked out for each other.

But Grammie had an aneurysm last month. A stomach aneurysm. I didn't know people could even get aneurysms in their
stomach. But she did.

And I've been alone for three weeks now.

There are reasons I'm leaving Nova Scotia.

You know how people say you can take a shell, and put it to your
ear and you'll hear the ocean?

When I drive out there now, out to Lawrencetown, and sit on
the beach . . . I can't hear it anymore. Not like I used to be able to.
That full sound is gone. The music is gone.

So I sit on the beach, and I try and pretend like I still hear it.

Just like when you take a shell and put it to your ear. You don't
really hear the ocean.

You just imagine you do. You pretend. Your brain lets you pretend you do.

I'm not listening to the ocean anymore. I'm listening to a shell,
because the only sounds that are left for me in Lawrencetown are
the imaginary ones in my head.

So maybe I just need to find another ocean. Take my tape
recorder with me and just . . . find that real sound again.

I could head to Tofino. I could take my grandmother's car and
drive there. I could be there in a couple of weeks.

There's even surfing at Tofino.
There's a whole different ocean there.
Take my tape recorder with me, fill my world back up again.
With real sounds again.

1.

SCOTT, 36 (HALIFAX, NS)

It was very hard—the first day I went back to work at the packaging plant—to try and get back into the swing of things. My body was all fresh and rested and ready to go, all of that was fine. It was more my whole mental state of mind, I realize now, that was not prepared. I was ready to go into the place and go to work; but at work, you know how there are some times . . . sometimes you can have these down periods? Well, we got to around two o'clock in the afternoon, my first day back, and everything started slowing down because we had been working so hard in the morning, and at around two o'clock, when stuff started slowing down . . . that's when everything really hit me. I'm talking about . . . the drag of what having a job again meant. Because I was stuck there. Stuck there with nothing to do, but I couldn't go home. I couldn't go home because I needed the hours, you know? The whole reason I was doing this for was for the money. I was being paid by the hour, so I couldn't leave for that. I wasn't allowed to leave anyway, just in case orders came in and everything picked back up. So I found myself stuck in this weird limbo for a while. This at-work limbo.

It never happens to me when I'm at home. That kind of feeling. I think it's because there's always something to do at home. Cleaning the bathroom or watering the avocado plant or clipping your toenails or even, at the very least, you can get away from your house and go for a walk. You can go outside. Watch the wind blowing through the trees or feel the sunlight baking your skin like the crust on a big meat pie. You can call a friend on your phone and shoot the shit. You can email somebody. You can watch YouTube.

When you're at work, though, you have to just stand around and cope with the downtime. Maybe you can try and start up a conversation with some person you just met. But, I mean, you don't really care about how many Dalmatians he's raising on his puppy farm or how his or her neighbours backed into their car by accident and how it's become this whole ordeal trying to get the insurance company to cover it. You don't give a shit that they're bored too. I mean, my co-workers . . . I don't give a shit about them. Not really. Not underneath it all. I don't give a shit about what they think about our current prime minister. I don't care what they think about the senate, and I don't want to hear them talk about their kids or their bills or how about nobody around here gets paid enough. I just want to do my work and go home. Get back to my real life. The life that I . . . choose.

Feels like a prison scenario, sometimes. Well, it is that, though. Oh hell, I don't know what I'm trying to say.

I understand the big picture of it all. I get that we gotta keep the big wheels spinnin'. This whole society thing moving. For some reason, right?

What was the reason, again?

Maybe what we're doin' is . . . by having jobs, by working at these places we don't really want to be connected to . . . maybe what we're doing is just dispersing the whole problem of downtime, you know?

Like, if the whole thing stopped . . . if the whole machine just stopped turning . . . I mean, the downtime you'd be left with that people would have to deal with would be . . . an impossible amount of downtime. Too much downtime. Enough downtime I don't think YouTube's servers could handle it. I don't think the outdoors could handle it. Planet Earth. And then everything would be hell. For everyone.

The big wheel, the machine . . . might be our answer to it, then, if that's the case. These constructed things, rituals are all part of our strategy to avoid . . . maybe this whole thing . . . maybe it's all this big avoidance technique or . . . I don't know.

You caught me in this odd mood. This unique time in my life. In transition.

I have a job again. I'm working again. I might not be myself because of it.

I should probably just shut up and be happy and accept it all. Except, no, because I still feel weird. Because last week I walked back into a packaging plant and now . . . everything's different again.

How does that happen?

What's happening to me?

And why am I going back there to do it all again tomorrow?

We labour to keep it bound.

The beast beneath it all.

Thanks for the ride, kid.

2.

PAUL, 45 (GREAT VILLAGE, NS)

We'd been out cutting hardwood all day, me and Danny Lavoie. Was late in the season, and we'd both been so busy that year with other stuff and stuff at work. Was a good year for construction, but both of our homes had wood furnaces, and so we were behind and both of us too proud, of course, to pay for someone else's reserves when we both had quality woodlots of our own.

When the cutting was done, chunks of maple and birch piled everywhere, it was getting 'round near six. The sky was turning orange and pink, and we knew we were gonna run out of daylight. So we started chucking wood as quick as we could into the back of the pickup, this GMC Sierra I'd had since my father had willed it to me, this old model he'd bought in the early eighties . . . and me and Danny, both of us old enough that we were starting to feel the fatigue of the day's worth of work on our muscles and bones.

Got the truck loaded up, jumped inside the cab, turned the key . . . and nothing. Turned the key again and nothin'. So I reached behind the seat, grabbed the claw hammer, got out of the cab, crawled under the thing and started banging away on the starter. I had Danny in the cab to keep trying the ignition . . . Thank Christ, after about fifteen minutes or so, I managed to knock the thing in just the right place, Danny turned the key, Sierra just roared to life, strong as anything. Just needed a tap in just the right spot.

When we got back to my place, I parked the Sierra and told Danny to go home; we could unload the wood tomorrow. We'd cut enough for the winter for both our houses, so we could do all the moving Sunday morning. He was as tired as me at that point, so that was all good and fine.

I went into the house, and Sarah was watching *Counterstrike* with Christopher Plummer on CTV. There were leftovers in the fridge from the past couple o' days, so I heated up some beans and some lasagne and brought it into the living room and ate while she snuggled up beside me. This had kind of become our routine at that point: I'd come home from workin', she'd already be watchin' TV. I'd cook something, and we'd either eat together, or I'd catch up on mine and we'd watch TV together until the late-night news came on. When the news came on, one of us usually would be falling asleep, and when one of us started falling asleep, the other one would wake the other up and we'd throw the dishes in the sink and brush our teeth and head upstairs to bed.

When we got into bed, that's when we'd talk. Usually about things that we'd found funny that day, or stuff that'd happened to one of our neighbours, or about whatever it was that was worrying us at that moment. And so, this night that I'm thinking about, this night I was trying to fall asleep. My blood was tired, and ever since I'd turned forty-eight or so, I'd have troubles staying awake for these late-night sessions. But Sarah, she was at me about somethin', somethin' that was worrying to her, somethin' that was annoyin' to me, 'cause I didn't have no answer for her about it . . . And the night before I'd fallen asleep on her when she was tryin' to have this conversation with me and . . . well, because I had gotten away with it the other night, I figured I could get away with it this night, too, and just kinda . . . fall asleep on her without . . . talking about it, I guess. Somethin' about destiny whatever, destiny and death or somethin'—

But then she touched me. Not in some kind of over-the-top exaggerated way like you see those idiot thirty-year-old actors in those MTV movies for kids . . . I mean . . . she touched me in a . . . this gentle kinda nudge. In just the right place. In just the right way.

And somethin' inside me just . . . snapped. Somethin' just . . . turned over inside of me. And all of a sudden I was awake again. All my fatigue was gone. My mind was clear and I . . . it was like I had had something inside of me . . . Somethin' inside of me all my life that had been sleeping. Something inside me that had just been waiting for this call.

So I grabbed her . . . hard, but with love. My eyes felt like flashlights, wide open, and I could see in the dark. And I could smell her. And I could hear her breath so clearly . . . so many nights before these things . . . I seemed to have had these things on mute or . . . like I had turned the volume down on her . . . but this night I was aware. She'd kick-started somethin' in me, and so I grabbed her and breathed her in and looked into her eyes in the dark. And then we paused. And then I kissed her, and she kissed me back. And I kissed her harder, and she grabbed my hair and . . .

We pulled into each other, and we wanted each other's weight, and we needed each other's heat. And our clumsiness didn't matter, and our bed didn't matter, and the house didn't matter. The bills didn't matter. The firewood didn't matter. The only thing that mattered to us was us. Being together. That was it.

Was a good night. Next thing I knew, I rolled over and looked at the clock, which read four forty-two in bright, red digital numbers. The window was open a crack and, when our panting slowed, we could hear the morning birds waking up in the darkness outside as we clenched each other.

And after a few more minutes of birdsong, and bliss . . . I started talking to her. And I don't know where they came from but . . . I had all the answers. All the answers to all the stuff that had been worrying her, all the answers to every question she'd ever asked me. And when I was done, she leaned over and kissed me. And fell asleep on my chest. Happy, it seemed. At peace. And I stayed real still, and I stayed real awake. Because I'd always wanted to be like that with her. I wanted to remember every moment. What was going to happen next?

Because after twenty-seven years of marriage, after all of the struggle and bullshit and hardship and distance I had ever put her through, this girl still wanted me. Her nudge, the way she had . . . that's what it made me realize. That's what brought me back into this life. Into this life with Sarah.

3.

HARLEY, 56 (PARRSBORO, NS)

It used to be you were supposed to be eighteen before you could get your licence, but I was sixteen at the time. I love drivin'. I been driving for forty years. I'm in my fifties now.

Yes, you're gettin' off lucky. You thought it was your transmission. If it had been your transmission, then you'd be in a pickle, eh? Then you'd be stuck here, right in Parrsboro. Could be worse! Could have broke down in Advocate or somewhere real off the beaten path. Transmission, that'd take us three or four days get a transmission for a Civic. Two-thousand-and-one, anyway. Axle, though, we might be able to help you. I might got one in the yard, that vehicle we got buried behind Phil Morris's truck, possibly. I'll get Dave on the loader. Yes, we might be able to fix ya up. Might have a spare axle around for a 2001.

Being a tow-truck driver, well . . . this job you meet all kinds of people. All kinds. You get your assholes. You certainly get those. But most people, they can be really nice.

That same corner your Civic was, on that same corner across the road last week this young fella, eh? Took 'er right off, lost control, totalled the fuckin' car. Not hurt at all. His car was a fuckin' write-off, but he was fine.

Then you would've been stuck, eh? If it was yer transmission. You saw me rollin' the thing back and forth while it was in park? That's how I knew. That's gotta be an axle.

Guy lost his life down the road here last week. Down near Fox River. That was a real mess. Lost his life. These roads, see. Speed. They can't drive 'em like us old guys can. But even considerin' that . . . there been a lot of accidents on this road lately. More than usual. Not sure what's going on.

Yeah, but you do meet some nice people. This gentleman and his wife, and this was years back now, they were up here, and their car broke down, and they were pretty impressed with me. He told her, once they were back down in the States, he told her, "Now look. If anything ever happens to me, you go up there to Nova Scotia and you settle with that Harley."

And it was years later and I'm at the salvage yard and who walks in, eh? His wife. The woman. From years before. She's happy to see me, we have a pleasant conversation . . . she was a nice lady. But, at the end of it, she started telling me, "Now, Harley, my husband said . . . " And she told me all about it. And how he'd told her to settle down with me. And so she asked me if I'd like to move with her to the States. And I said, "The States? What about your husband?" And then she told me her husband had passed on. And she wanted me to move down with her, eh?

Don't get me wrong, nice people. Down in the States. Nice place to visit. Nice and everything. But here is where I was born. My father, he told me: Harley, you want anything in this life, you better be prepared to work your guts out for it. That's why I work the crazy hours, see? Six a.m. to midnight. I don't stop, either, eh? I like workin'. Work ethic, I got a good work ethic . . . that's why I can always find work, eh? I don't stop.

I used to just go from town to town. Ten days working for someone here, then I'd move on. Didn't like staying anywhere too long. But I could always find work. One time I was in Ontario, this town, this asshole got pissed off at me that I had worked only a week for him. "You'll never get work in this town again," he said. So I looked at him and said, "What do you mean?" And he looked at me and said, "You leave now, you'll never get any work in this town again." And so I asked him, "Well, how do you think you're gonna manage that?"

"Never you mind," he said, "but, you quit now, you'll never work in this town again."

So I walked out of his office and across the street to this lumber yard and went inside and talked to the boss there and told him I'd like to start driving trucks for him and that this asshole across the street was giving me trouble. I said, "Can I work for you as a driver?" And he said, "Yes you can, sir!"

And so I went back across the road to the asshole, see, and I told him that I got a job. And he was pissed. And then I said, "I'd like my severance pay now." And the asshole said, "I'm not paying you a goddamned cent!" And I said, "Okay!" And so I walked down the hallway and into the secretary's office and I told her that I was ready to move on, and I asked her if I could I have my severance cheque. And she said, "Sure you can, sir." And she gave it to me.

And so I walked back into the asshole's office, and I told him I just got my severance cheque and that I was done. And he asked me, "How'd you get that severance cheque?"

And so I ran out of there, fast as I could, out the door and down the street to the bank and told the bank cashier to cash the cheque real quick because this guy had a reputation for cancelling cheques to his employees. And no sooner had she handed me the money than the bank's phone started ringing. And it was the asshole. Asking about cancelling the cheque. But it had already gone through, see? And I had a lovely time the next two weeks working for the gentleman at the lumber company. Yes, he was a nice employer, he was.

That lady from the States, she called me again a couple of years ago, askin' me if I'd come visit her. Trying to get me to go down, eh? It's a nice place, don't get me wrong.

You're pretty lucky; it was just the axle. If it was your transmission, then you'd be fucked.

You can smoke in the cab here. I get nasty about it only if there's a lady present. If there's a lady present, that's different. We can smoke now, though.

Anything built by man ain't perfect. Nobody on this earth does anything one hundred percent, eh? That's mankind. Don't feel bad. No one in the world does anything one hundred percent.

We'll get you back on the road. If we got the part. Shouldn't take very long. If we got the part.

4.

JIM, 28 (AMHERST, NS)

It's just been a quiet summer, you know?

I wasn't expecting it to be. I figured we'd be busy. Heart attacks or D.U.I. victims, the usual. We get a lot of joyriders, drinking and driving out in this area. A lot of seniors live here too, so . . . well, you know how it goes, right?

But so far it's been quiet. Really. Which is nice.

The spot where we park the ambulance is out in the middle of nowhere of course. Side of the road. In the trees. Waiting for the call.

They can be pretty long nights, sometimes.

We always stock up on Tim Hortons before we go out there. Me and whomever I'm partnered with for the shift. Bring a book or whatnot. To eat up the time.

Pretty quiet, except for the crickets. Or cicadas. Probably not cicadas, they don't live around here, right? More like crickets. But maybe not crickets. What's the type of insect that makes that noise? You know the one I mean. Not the cricket chirping but that steady, buzzy drone? That sound. Hear that a lot out here. I mean, crickets too, but also that drone.

Crosswords, I got really into crosswords, at one point. The last one I tried to complete . . . I got stuck on this one word . . . four-letter word for passion. This was October of last year. Four-letter word for passion. Couldn't figure out if they were looking for zeal or rage. I figured it had to be either zeal or rage. The word was situated in this empty corner of the puzzle, and I hadn't gotten around to solving the words around it yet. But for some reason I got stuck on that one. Could not proceed. Then we got the call. A car had driven off the road and hit a tree. Ten kilometres south of us. We responded to the call.

She was dead when we got there. She had a baby with her, in the car. Baby was fine. Crying, but . . . yeah, okay other than that. She hadn't been wearing her seat belt. She didn't have her head when we found her body. That was . . . metres away. Her eyes were still open. On her head. The investigator arrived, and he couldn't quite figure out how she got like that. I was the one who found her. My partner that night, Bruno Lapointe, he was checking on the kid, and I walked into the woods with my light. Her body didn't bug me. But, when the beam of my flashlight landed on the rest of her, the light kind of made her eyes gleam at me. Kind of like, sparkled. That kind of well . . . threw me, you could say.

I'd seen worse before. But somethin' about that moment when I first found her and saw her and how her eyes kind of sparkled . . .

Once everything was cleaned up, and we took care of everything and run into town and dropped off the body and then back to Tim Hortons and then back out to our parking spot in the trees, Bruno started making these jokes about people losin' their heads and everything and . . . dismemberment jokes, see? There are lots of jokes about dismemberment. How people can sometimes actually lose pieces of themselves. And we make jokes sometimes . . . When you're a paramedic sometimes . . . helps us deal with stuff. It's not the craziest of behaviours for people who deal with what we deal with day in, day out, all right?

But Bruno was kind of being relentless with them that night, so at one point I had to just excuse myself to have a cigarette. And I remember hopping out of the ambulance and taking a few steps and just staring up at the night in the sky. Just staring up at the night in the sky and listening to the crickets and cicadas or whatever.

And the sky became . . . in the sky I could have sworn I could see the crossword puzzle I was working on earlier. Almost like as if it were a constellation or something. And I could see that empty corner. And I could see seventy-two across . . . four blank spaces. A four-letter word for passion.

I still couldn't figure out if the answer was zeal or rage.
I never did another crossword after that.
I don't know why.
The drone doesn't bug me so much.

5.

LORI, 64 (AULAC, NB)

I'll give ya my opinion. Now, it's just an opinion and if ya don't like it, you can just ignore me. Because, ya see, what I think is that it's just life as per usual. Someone comes up with this idea. Some entrepreneurial type. Is yer coffee okay, dear? Is it cold? I could fetch ya a warmer. It'd just take a second. I can zip right over the counter here and . . . ya sure?

So why can't ya talk in the interview? Rick Mercer, he talks in all his interviews. Most of the time he talks more than the person he's interviewing. Of course, that's just a spoof show, I guess. Or a fake news show. Ya know what I mean. Yeah? Blink twice if ya know what I mean. Ha! No, I'm just kidding. I'm just giving ya a hard time. I'll be good. I'm very good, actually. I'm a very good person. I don't stir people up. I just take their orders and bring them their food and take away their plates and hand them their bills and run them through the cash register. I work a regular week, and I'm very thankful for my work, this job, and my life outside of this job with my dog and my husband, and I've always been very good. Because ya should be good, you know what I mean? People appreciate it when yer good. When ya don't treat them like a . . . ya-know-what. Arsehole. This is life as per usual. This is how it works. Or how it should work. Everyone should treat each other with respect and . . .

But then you get these entrepreneurial types, and, one day, they might come up with some idea in their head. Some crazy new way for how to make money. So they work their butts off trying to get this idea of theirs goin'. Trying to get it off the ground. Like a kite. They try and get their kite off the ground. The kite is their idea.

Their idea becomes their company. And so they—them—they try and get it off the ground themselves, at first. And they gotta run real fast to get it going, you know. To get it up there. Get it up and flying. And it takes a lot out of them. Trying to get their kite up there. And sometimes, the kite crashes right off the bat. No matter how hard they run, these entrepreneurial types. But sometimes, sometimes they get lucky, and they run and the kite goes up and suddenly, the wind grabs it! And then, all of a sudden, the kite is flying in the sky, high in the sky . . . except now these entrepreneurial types are tired from all the running they had to do themselves. Trying to get the kite up in the air. They need to take a break. So they decide they need someone to keep running the kite for them. Just for a little while. Just until they get their breath back.

So the entrepreneur, they hire someone because now they can. Because of the kite. Because the kite isn't actually a kite. It's an idea. It's a money-making machine.

And the entrepreneur becomes the boss. And pretty soon, the boss gets tired of taking turns running the kite with his employee. And since they've been running the kite steady like they have, the boss starts thinking, "Why should I run the kite at all? Jeesh, I could just hire another guy and never have to run the kite again and still make all this money."

Ya get what I'm sayin'?

The entrepreneur starts out flying the kite, right? But the next step after flying the kite, is taking a step away from the kite. And the next step after that is taking another step away from the kite. And then, another step and another step, and the next thing you know, the entrepreneur is sitting in a rocking chair on his porch over a mile away, watching his kite flying in the distance. And his life is completely different than the lives of the people actually flying that blessed kite now. Flying it for him. Weird how it works, right?

The guy who started these gas stations, he ain't even alive no more. His sons run the business now. They're the ones who own everything. They own all the gas stations, the restaurants like this one, the gift shops, the oil refineries offshore, all the local newspapers, half of all the forests everywhere, and who knows where they are right now? . . . on their porches somewhere . . . but I'm the one flying the kite. Ya get me? I'm the one running that cash register.

And this is how it is. How it's gotta be.

I been doing this . . . five years now. I used to work in a fish plant. Ya couldn't get the scent of the work off of ya at the end of the day.

Ya want me to fetch you a warmer for yer coffee?

I've met my share of pleasant people. I've met some not-so-pleasant ones, too.

But I've always been very good.

6.

VICKI, 21 (SACKVILLE, NB)

Hello, my name is Vicki Lawson, and I am a student attending Mount Allison University, here in Sackville, New Brunswick. I am studying music. I'm a cellist, which means I play the cello. The cello is a musical instrument.

I'm not really sure what to say. What do you want me to say?

You just want me to talk? About anything?

Okay. Well. My name is Vicki Lawson, and I am a music student . . . I already said that.

Did you notice that everything in this town is named after ducks? Like the café down the street. The Black Duck? And this bar we're in? Ducky's? Everything's named after ducks.

I mean, I know the town's right beside that big duck pond. Marsh. Lake. Whatever. But what is the big deal? Really. What is the big deal? Have some originality, people. Like, have some friggin' originality.

Not everything's gotta have a duck in its name. Or be named after the ducks. If I ever open up a business here in Sackville, I'm not going to call it anything to do with ducks. I'm going to call it . . . Vicki's. I'm not going to call it the Duck Emporium. Or the Duck Pond. Or the Pyramid of Ducks. I'm going to call it Vicki's.

I might be the worst person in town you could have interviewed. I don't really have that much to say.

I like music. I like playing cello. It makes me happy. The cello is . . . I don't know . . . deep. I guess. The sound of it . . . the sound of deep. Deep and rich, and fluid. A moving sound. Like the ocean. Not like a pond. Not shallow and static and dead and full of duck shit.

You kind of stink. I think it's you. Yes, it's you. You stink. When was the last time you showered?

Your hair is greasy.

I don't think I could ever do what you are doing. Backpacking. I couldn't do it. I would need hotels, if I was travelling. Hotels and showers. And deodorant.

Sorry. It is kind of funny though. You smell like an old sock.

What do you think about that?

Nothing? You don't have anything to say for yourself?

I'll make you crack. I will make you crack.

You smell like a duck's rotten asshole. You smell like . . .

You smell like a homeless guy. You smell lost. You smell like no one has ever loved you.

Has anyone ever loved you? Have you ever been in love with anyone?

I was in love with someone once. Here. Last semester. My third year. He cheated on me with another musician. A percussionist. That little drummer bitch.

She smelled like a duck's rotten asshole. She didn't shower. She smelled like a homeless guy.

No one had ever loved her before. That's how she could justify it. Sleeping with another girl's boyfriend.

He ran off with her. He didn't withdraw from his courses or anything. She was just a passing-through dirty musician. I found out because they left a note.

There was a quote in the note.

"In dreams, the truth is learned that all good works are done in the absence of a caress."

It was a Leonard Cohen quote.

I don't know what he meant by it. What he was inferring. And I don't care to know. But now I don't know what to think. Of Leonard Cohen anymore. Of Leonard Cohen, or of this place. Or of all these ducks. Or of people who don't shower.

Or of myself. I don't even know what to think of myself anymore.

And every duck, every musician, every person who doesn't shower reminds me of that fact, eventually.

You stink. Did you hear me when I told you that you stink?
You stink.
But you didn't crack.
Good job.
You don't smell that bad.

JULY

LOWELL (MONCTON, NB)

The Civic broke down in Parrsboro. I've been hitchhiking since then. Hitchhiking is a crazy experience. I didn't expect it to be so . . . uh . . . because the guy who drove me from the Sackville off-ramp to here, he asked me for . . . for a blowjob. I told him I wasn't interested, that I wasn't going to give him one. That pissed him off. He demanded I give him gas money instead. So I gave him twenty bucks. Sometimes you gotta be proactive with setting up boundaries with people, I guess.

There's this whole other side to humanity out there.

Like part of a sound you can't hear. Streaming through these interactions. Signals being transmitted on some kind of weird frequency. You can't quite hear it, but you know it's there. Underneath everything. Animalistic. A feeling of teeth and muscles tensing.

Not everyone I've come across has been super-responsive about being interviewed, either. Some people just politely refuse, but I've had a lot of people tell me to "Fuck off," or "Go fuck myself," or "Get the fuck out of here." There's a lot of stuff that doesn't make it onto the tapes. Sounds that don't want to be captured.

I'm in Moncton sitting down in this café called the Laundromat. Everyone here is speaking French, and my French isn't the greatest, so I can't really tell what the other customers are talking about. It's like I've walked into some kind of foreign movie or something.

I'm drinking a pint of craft beer right now, and I have no idea what craft beer even is. I don't even know what the bartender just said to me. I just said "Oui" a couple of times and gave him a ten-dollar bill. He just kind of looked at me funny and poured me this pint. It tastes all right, I guess. But I really need to eat something.

Maybe a poutine or something. Maybe a donair.

Tofino is six thousand kilometres away.

1.

MARK, 35 (DIEPPE, NB)

I tell her, I say, "Janey, don't worry about so much what Joseph says. No, I don't care what he thinks. If I don't care what he thinks, then why should you care what he thinks? Well, ya shouldn't, for cryin' out loud." But she does anyway. And I know why.

Joseph, well, he's gotta couple of screws loose, that's for sure. But he's real sharp about lots of other stuff. He knows what's goin' on in the world . . . I mean, not in all of the world. Nobody knows what's goin' on in *all* of the world. I mean, he couldn't tell you what the Greeks are up to, over in Greece. Or what the Israelites are doing to each other . . . but then again, he would have his theories about them . . . and the theories, more often than not, would be real close to a kind of unsaid truth . . . the stuff that people never talk about . . . the stuff that's so deep down, we don't even admit it as truth kind of stuff. Joseph comes real close to figurin' out a lot of that unsaid truth. He's got a sharp nose for it. That's why Janey's scared. She figures there's something that Joseph sees that we can't, as far as tryin' to have a kid's concerned. Somethin' under the surface. Somethin' he sees, but won't tell us about.

Maybe she's worried because she thinks Joseph thinks I'm not committed to her. That I'll cheat on her. Maybe I think Joseph thinks the same about her. But her eyes don't wander. Neither do mine. So what does Joseph see? What does he see, but we can't? What is he not tellin' us about? And that's how and why the argument comes around. That's why I'm trying to hold her while she's trying to push me away. Me hearin' myself say, "Janey. Don't worry so much." And she's tellin' me she can't help it. And I say, "I know. I know you can't but . . . "

But.

All the time both of us wishin' things were different.

Which is funny because we don't actually wish anything were different at all. I want to be with her. And, for the rest of my life, I want to be with her. And her, I'm pretty sure she wants to be my girl, be with me for the rest of my life. And neither one of us wants to move. We both wanna live here, even though it can be shitty weather, and our apartment's not in the best neighbourhood, and the building we're in's fallin' apart and everything. Our family's close by. Joseph's close.

But we get our heads and our hearts all tied up in knots a lot of the time and find ourselves wishing things were different. And by that, I mean different in ways we don't even know. Like crazy different, but the same. Like the same, just . . . maybe if we won the lotto or somethin'. And that would be the kind of different that would help. We'd still live in town, still stay close to the family . . . but we wouldn't be in so much debt, and we wouldn't have to worry so much about what we were spending on groceries so much every single damn time we walk into the grocery store. That's all I mean by different. We just wish . . . well . . . that everything could be like it is . . . just . . . not having to worry about all of this other stuff that seems outside of us. What is actually us. Because being poor isn't . . . us. We don't feel poor, you know? But we're living poor. And that pressure . . . the feeling of that pressure, I mean . . . that's what aggravates all of this other subconscious fear and worry and bullshit that we keep feelin'.

Joseph . . . for as smart and sharp as he is, he don't . . . gotta worry about that. His wife, Janey's mom, she's dead. He's living la vie compl=tement seul. By himself. He's gotta pay for his own cheese and lobster meat, and that's it. All retired with his pension and . . .

Trying to take the pressure off of us, trying to keep the stress away from Janey . . . it's killing me. I can't find a job around here that pays more than twelve bucks an hour. I had a job with a moving company last year that was great, all under-the-table stuff, but then the guy who owned the truck threw out his back and became a coke-head on his downtime and never got the business up and running again. I guess that's another way you can retire.

And retirement? Not for me. I won't be able to . . . retire. So there's the pressure of that on top of everything.

It takes something to be in a relationship. It takes something to keep them going. But the world ain't turning in a right way to keep people together. The world's spinnin' . . . sure, it's spinning, but it's spinning us all apart.

This week, I gotta find a way to come up with six hundred and fifty more dollars for rent. By Friday. Forty eight hours from now. You tell me how that's gonna happen, right?

I mean, you tell me.

Because I got nothin'.

And I'm gonna lose everything.

And it makes me want to say, "Fuck Joseph." Even though I love him.

And it makes me want to leave my girl. Even though I love her.

But the world's spinning me apart.

What's funny is, back when I was still workin' . . . with the movers? Most of the people we moved, it was breakups. I mean, mostly. People going through divorces or . . . breakin' up. It's happenin' everywhere, all the time. It's happenin' now. Two streets over from here. That apartment building down the road. That duplex over on Benoit. Maybe even in that shithole across the street.

Yah.

2.

SANDRA, 43 (RIVERVIEW, NB)

I don't know what I'm doing right now. Talking to you. I spend all day talking to people. I spend all day talking to people I don't know. I don't know how you managed to . . . get me to talk to you.

It's probably because I'm too tired to try and get away from you. Or make up some excuse as to why I can't. Talk to you.

I follow a script at work, when I handle all the incoming calls. People looking for rental cars.

I kind of like the script in a way. I can autopilot my way through the day, sometimes.

The tricky ones, the people with all of the pent-up rage issues, they can be tough. But I just refer back to the script to get through them.

The hardest is when you get an American with a really thick accent. From the southwest. They can be tough to understand, for me, sometimes. Sometimes they talk really slow, too, and you just kind of have to wait for them to finish their sentences. That can be a bit annoying. Funny thing about Americans though: The thicker their accent, the more polite they are. At least over the phone. At least, in my experience. I guess my experience could be a lot different than other people's. But that's why you're recording me, isn't it? To get my unique perspective.

I like talking to people. I do. It's just after ten straight hours of doing it, you kind of get a little pooped from doing it.

It can be tiring.

But it can get kind of addictive, too, I guess.

I have a cat at home.

I don't really have a lot of social friends. Most of my social friends have moved away. Got married or for other reasons.

My mother, she lives in town.

My cat doesn't really make any noise. His name is Pete. Pete doesn't purr. He doesn't mew. He doesn't meow. He's silent. He does his own thing, and he's silent. When he wants something . . . say, if I've forgotten to feed him, he just sticks his claws into my feet. Or he stares at me. Sometimes I'll wake up and he'll be sitting on my chest just staring at me, but not purring or anything. I thought that most cats purred, don't they?

So, in an odd way . . . the Americans looking to reserve their rental cars . . . they're kind of a relief. Even though they're exhausting. They make me feel . . . normal. When they talk to me. Answer my questions. Even if they're having a fit on the phone. Sometimes I can even make small talk, not related to rentals.

And I get to hear about the weather in Henderson, Texas. And what people in Cicero, Illinois, are thinking about the latest election campaign. What some lady in Anaconda, Montana, had for breakfast.

All of these voices coming at me through my earpiece, all this chatter, and, when I get home, there's nothing. Pete is a very quiet cat.

I must be one of the strange ones, yeah? That you've interviewed? Lady tells you she's tired of talking to people, then five seconds later, she's telling you the opposite.

People are paradoxical, though. At least they're not silent.

3.

SEANA, 25 (HILLSBOROUGH, NB)

I haven't made it down to the rocks yet this summer. We've been out to Parlee Beach a couple of times already. My boyfriend took me down to Lawrencetown two weeks ago because he's big into surfing, too, but we haven't gone down to the Rocks yet. They are nice, though.

You can just have that coffee, okay? I'm not going to charge you for just a coffee. If you get a sandwich or anything, I'll have to charge you for that. The coffee I can just write off. I pretty much drink an entire pot myself on one of these shifts anyway. I'm addicted to the stuff, I can't help it anymore.

There aren't that many jobs here in the town, so I'm just happy I don't have to drive into Moncton every day. Not crazy about Moncton. I mean it's all right. It's not my favourite place in the world. I like Halifax better. Well, I don't even really like Halifax that much, but I like Lawrencetown. I guess I just don't like cities that much, even though you can't really call them cities. Here in the Maritimes. I mean, I went to Montreal for my first year of university, before I dropped out and came back. Montreal is a city. You should totally hit Montreal, if you're just travelling. Go to Schwartz's. Schwartz's smoked meat sandwiches. I wish I was eating a smoked meat sandwich from Schwartz's. Our sandwiches are all right. Our roast beef is okay. But I make them every morning at the start of the shift, and all the ingredients, I mean, the owner just buys the ingredients from the grocery store down the street here, and there's nothing gourmet about them. Ooh, and a black cherry pop to go with it. The smoked meat sandwich. That would be awesome.

We're usually a lot busier than this. There haven't been as many tourists yet this season. Tourist season has been going slow, usually there's a few people in here. More people passing through, normally.

People are staying a bit more put this year. Sometimes everyone waits until August to hit the Maritimes. I don't know that for a fact; that's just what I seem to recall hearing.

There was a guy, though, came through last week . . . he liked the roast beef sandwich I made so much, he tipped me twenty dollars. I wasn't sure if he had done it on purpose, though, because who tips twenty dollars for a sandwich? I mean he had a coffee, too, but still. The coffee we get here, it's the same type of coffee you'd get at a gas station. It's nothing special. It's on par with gas station coffee. Which is really just a small step up from drinking motor oil. I do put care into the sandwiches, though. Even though the ingredients are just from the store down the road.

Anyway, he had tipped me twenty dollars, so I was like, "Oh, excuse me, sir. I think you might have made a mistake. This is a twenty-dollar bill." And he kind of looked at me funny, and he was all like, "Yeah." But I couldn't really read him, so I had to keep at him to figure him out. So I was like, "I'm sorry, it's a twenty-dollar bill, is what I mean." And he said, "Spend it while you still can." But he had stopped looking at me at this point, and was already turned away and moving toward the door.

He was dressed in an all-black suit and his hair was all slicked back. And his skin was so tan he was almost orange. And he never took his sunglasses off. The whole time he was here. And so I was just standing there holding this twenty-dollar bill in my hand and staring at his back, watching him walk away, with my mouth, it must have been a little bit open, you know. And when he got to the door, he turned around, and he saw me staring at him, with my mouth open and the twenty-dollar bill in my hand. And his eyebrows, they kind of bunched up . . . no . . . what's that word . . . furrowed. His brows furrowed, and he didn't know what was wrong with me, and he said, "What." Just like that. "What." And he smiled. I think it was a smile. He had weird teeth.

And so I just said, "Oh! Nothing! Have a good day!" And I was about to say something else but he was already out the door and halfway to his car before I could blink.

I don't know what he meant by the whole "spend-it-while-you-still-can" business. But, still, I got tipped twenty dollars for a friggin' roast beef sandwich.

So after I closed up the café, I walked right down the street to the Scotiabank, put it right into an envelope and deposited it right into my account.

Someday I'm going to travel to Portugal. The Portuguese coast? All these beautiful little fishing villages along the Portuguese coast. Me and my boyfriend, we've been planning it ever since we hooked up.

You know what the word for beautiful is in Portuguese? Bonito.

So I know I make good sandwiches. That's the trick, you know? To everything. Figuring out how to make something awesome out of just regular stuff.

Like my sandwiches. My sandwiches are bonito.

4.

WALLACE, 55 (HOPEWELL, NB)

If those fuckin' wingnuts come around here again, I'll fill their asses full of birdseed. And by birdseed I mean buckshot. And by buckshot, I mean bullets. Last time they came, they knocked on my door and asked permission. I told them to go to hell. That's why they didn't ask this time. That's why they parked down the road a ways, edge of the property, this time.

You know who I'm talkin' about. The guys in the suits! Those sunburnt cocksucker suit-wearin' pricks! The ones with the sunglasses! I'll knock the goddamned sunglasses from their faces if they try and trespass on my land again!

Poking around all over my fuckin' . . . the land was given to my great, great, great, fuckin' great, great grandfather by the Crown for being a good fuckin' loyalist. Passed down generation to generation, hand to hand of my kin over the course of two hundred odd fuckin' years!

God knows what they're lookin' for. They said they wanted to do an egg count of the birds down there. But that was bullshit. They said they were with the Department of Natural Resources. That was definitely bullshit. Department of Natural Resource guys don't dress like that.

And even if they were from the Department of Natural Resources . . . what the hell do they care about the fuckin' egg count of those birds down there, the fuckin' Guillemots? Why the hell does the government care? Not just countin' the guillemot eggs but also keeping track of the fuckin' number of children everybody has, the number of guns I got in my basement . . . like some giant fuckin' perverted supercomputer! Like some Peeping Tom calculator device—

Leave the fuckin' birds alone! Down along the cliffs! Stay outta their fuckin' nests and leave them alone! Like the guillemots don't have enough problems they gotta beak through!

I got my back brace now. I can shoot this fuckin' rifle now. If they start up with their tramplin' through my bushes again. Hey, you fuckin' wingnut cocksuckers! Whoever you are! You sickos! Leave the fuckin' birds alone! Just leave them—

End of tape FW-722B3.

5.

FINN, 68 (ALMA, NB)

So it's on, and I'm being recorded right now? I'm being recorded? Am I being recorded? Nod your head if I'm being . . .

So you're familiar with the area? You been out to the Hopewell Rocks, yes? Yes? Have you been out there or not? Nod your head or shake it. Nod your head for "yes" or shake it for "no." If you've been out to them. The Rocks. Yes? You've been out to them? Yes? All right, then. They're pretty, aren't they? They're pretty. And they got enough people working out there now, you don't get so many idiot tourists getting stuck out there anymore.

What about Cape Enrage? You been out to Cape Enrage? Yes? Was that a yes? Yes? I see. Quite the spectacle out there, isn't it? Were you out there when that fog crept up on us yesterday? Were you out to the cape when that fog crept up? Eh? Yes or no? You're nodding, yes? So, yes. Comes in quick, doesn't it? The fog. One second you're under the sun and a clear blue sky and then the next you're cutting through pea soup. Pea-soup fog. Thick fog.

That always used to spook me when I was younger. Growing up here. Whenever I was out that way. Either hayin' or ridin' my bike. My chums and me. We'd ride out there to goof around or whatever. Sometimes that fog would overtake us like . . .

It just swoops in. And you can see it coming at ya. How fast it moves. This wall of white. White mist. God knows what's in it. And it's movin' so fast, it just overtakes ya. And you know it's going to. The fog here is like fate. You know you can't outrun it. We could never keep ahead of it on our bikes. You can keep ahead of it in a car nowadays, but that's about it. Inescapable fate. Or fog. I'm talking about the fog right now.

And as a kid, there was the regular everyday world, and then there was the fog world. Almost like it was the reverse of the everyday world, fog world was. And the instant the fog wall overtook you, everything around you would be this thick, white air, and . . . it felt like the rules were all-of-a-sudden different, you know. There were different rules at play in fog world. Anything could happen. So you had to watch your back. Proceed with caution.

Proceed with caution so as you didn't, by accident, fall off the cliffs of Cape Enrage, like some idiot tourist. And look over your shoulder to make sure your friends hadn't either. Look over your shoulder to make sure your friends hadn't disappeared on ya, and look over your shoulder for boogeymen.

Because the boogeymen, they live in the fog, I'm sure you've heard. We all knew that as kids.

I never ran into them, personally. The boogeymen.

That's the reason why I got to grow up and become so old. They never got me.

They did get one of my chums, though.

Donnie. Donnie Clutterbuck.

They got him.

When we were eleven. Well, I was eleven, anyway. I think he was eleven, too. Long time ago, can't really remember all the specifics.

Donnie was bigger than the rest of us. And slower than the rest of us, too.

We were biking in a group, out to the cape, and the wall of fog rushed us. What year was that, now? 1958? Think I got the math right on that. 1958, yuh. There was a fella wrote a history of the town a couple of years back, he wrote about this story. But I'm pretty sure it happened in 1958.

Donnie was slower than the rest of us, though. And the fog, it overtook us. But we were real close to where we were going. To meet the rest of our friends. So me and Matthew and Thomas, we did not proceed with caution. We sped our bikes up. To get there quicker. And we did not look back over our shoulders. To make sure our friends were still there.

And by the time we got to the meeting spot, we noticed Donnie Clutterbuck wasn't with us anymore. And we waited for him and he never came.

And we called out his name, and he never answered. And the fog melted off.

And he was nowhere to be found.

And they formed a search party for him the next day.

And he was nowhere to be found.

And the men in the boats combed the coastline of the cliff base for him.

And he was nowhere to be found.

And his bike was never found either.

Because the boogeymen that live in the fog took him.

And I remember that. Thinking that when I was a kid.

Do you believe in the boogeymen? Nod your head yes if you do, or shake your head no if you don't.

Was that a nod or a shake?

Donnie Clutterbuck.

6.

ADAM, 44 (FUNDY NATIONAL PARK, NB)

My name is Adam. Robinson. And I am . . . waiting for my dog to show back up. I came here two days ago, for the weekend, with my dog, whose name is Hank . . . he's a Labrador retriever and pretty good at not running off, usually, so that's kind of part of the reason why I'm a bit freaking out right now. I'm not freaking out. I'm calm. He is coming back. Anytime now.

I called in to work tonight to let them know I'm not going to be in tomorrow morning. I got here on Friday, now it's Sunday and it's . . . seven p.m., and so even if I left now, I won't reach Sussex until nine . . . another two hours basically to Woodstock, so I wouldn't be getting home until eleven or almost midnight, I don't know, and I really don't want to leave here without my dog.

I first got the dog when me and my girlfriend at the time, now my ex-girlfriend . . . got the dog to try and . . . thought getting a dog would maybe . . . I don't know, cheer my girlfriend up but it just kind of pissed her off that I would get a dog when getting a dog really wasn't addressing any of the problems we were going through at the time.

I kind of had an honesty problem with her. About money. I would spend money . . . on things other than bills. Like, cigarettes and beer and stuff, and then I would lie about it, and she started catching me in these lies, and next thing I knew she was so sick of me . . . so sick of being lied to that there wasn't really anything I could say anymore to fix anything between us. So I went to the pet store and bought Hank. Which pissed my girlfriend (now ex-girlfriend) off even more because "this doesn't solve anything between us, and we needed that money for the power bill and . . . " You get the story, yeah?

So I had just got this dog. And I was kind of in this emotional place. Because I wasn't sure if I could be trusted to take care of anyone. Or be in a relationship with anyone. And I . . . I was a big mess. Vulnerable. I was very . . . vulnerable.

And I think the dog sensed that. And I think the dog really capitalized on that.

I mean, Hank . . . is great. Hank sleeps on the bed, sits on the couch with me, I mean, Hank is like a person. Except he's better than a person really, because I never have to lie to him, he never asks me what I've done with the money that was supposed to go to the power bill, and I mean, he eats way less than my ex-girlfriend ever did, so I'm saving a lot on groceries really. Because I mean, I can live off of frozen pizza and Kraft Dinner and I'm fine, you know?

And I can talk to Hank. Hank is there for me. And he listens. I mean, maybe he doesn't always understand what I'm saying, but I don't need to be understood. I never needed to be understood. I never wanted to be understood. I just wanted someone to listen to me and love me and that's it. Hang out and watch *Game of Thrones* with me.

The thing about people is . . . people are too intense for other people. Everything's got to be . . . hard truth and total honesty, and it's all got to be expressed in words and in blood and in writing, every single moment of your free time accounted for in a ledger, every single action, every word, every emotion, every feeling.

With dogs, you can be truthful, and they don't need it in writing, and they don't hold it against you for the rest of your life and make judgments about you and tell all their friends about how much of a liar you are and . . .

But Hank went missing on Friday night.

You got to keep your dog on a leash in the park. It's a rule. You're not supposed to leave them unsupervised. You're not supposed to. But I had to take a shit. What was I going to do, take him into the shitter with me? So I left him tied up to a tree beside the tent. The washroom of course, I got assigned the campsite furthest away from the frigging washrooms in the whole place. And I had to take a shit, which I don't like . . . rushing. The bowel stuff.

Came back and no Hank. The leash looks like something chewed through it. I don't know why Hank would chew through his own leash.

Talked to the park staff, they said they'll keep an eye out for him. That was Friday night.

Nothing yesterday. No Hank. Went to the park office, they haven't seen anything. No one has.

I figured dogs were great because they're not like people. They don't just up and leave you. Not like people.

And out of the blue. Like people, too. My girlfriend just left one day because she couldn't stand me. Hank just . . . bit through his leash Friday night.

Maybe I should have taken him to the shitter with me?

I couldn't sleep last night. Kept hearing these weird noises in the woods. Probably just normal noises for anyone who knows anything about the wilderness, but, for me, they were weird.

Like night birds or something.

I can't take Tuesday off work. If I take more than one day off at a time they won't like it. I don't have any clout there.

I just want Hank to come back.

I think I don't want to be recorded anymore, okay?

AUGUST

LOWELL (SUSSEX, NB)

Was on my way out of Fundy National, trying to hitchhike . . . but it took a while before anyone picked me up. I walked past this campground called Wolfe Lake. And I don't know why, but all of a sudden I started getting these weird ideas. I started thinking about wolves. And I just had this urge to write everything down. Get everything on paper. All of these ideas swirling together in my brain about these imaginary wolves. So I sat down on this big rock by the road, and I started writing about this family of wolves. This is what I wrote:

One night, our pack wandered onto a derelict plot. Farmland long forgotten and overrun with weeds. Our eyes gleamed in the night. We found a way into the house through a gap in a boarded up window. On the wooden floor of a ghost's kitchen we settled in. Cabo's stomach was getting worse, he whimpered as he slept. Outside in the darkness crickets and frogs and owls sang songs to each other. I couldn't stop thinking about my mother, and the blood on her coat when we found her the day after the desperate ones attacked.

That's all I got so far. I'm not sure what to do with it. But it's a fun . . . distraction.

Eventually this old Acadian couple picked me up and gave me a ride. They dropped me off at the Tim Hortons here in Sussex. I'm drinking coffee right now, recording this.

Sussex looks like it's all farmland and farmers and farms. Cows. A lot of cows. Rolling hills and tractors and pickup trucks.

But I bet there's a lot more to it than that.

Let's go find some noise.

1.

MARY, 72 (SUSSEX, NB)

I'm seventy-two and, my Lord, I still get spooked from time to time.

Just this past weekend, in fact. My daughter and her friend Lisa took me out to dinner, and they took me out into the country to this German food hall out in the sticks. It's out in the middle of nowhere, and you'd think those Germans were out of their minds building a restaurant out in the middle of nowhere like that. But it's where their farm is, see. They raise all of the animals themselves and butcher the meat themselves. They have their own butchery on the farm, also. So it makes sense in that regard. But you wonder how anyone ever manages to find their way out there. But the trick is, their food is that good. Those Germans are good cooks. I had a sausage out there and, my Lord, that sausage was bigger than my head! And good! Mmm-mmm-mmm! They make good food in their restaurant, those Germans.

But it's out in the middle of nowhere! It's a wonder anyone can even find the place. You have to drive out to the middle of nowhere, then you turn left and keep going. Out into the real middle of nowhere. Nothing but forest and farmland and covered bridges.

But their food is so good. It's worth it. It takes a while to get out there, but it's worth it.

But I'm seventy-two years young, and that doesn't seem to make any difference. I still can get spooked from time to time.

My daughter and her friend Lisa, Lisa was driving. They're one of those forward . . . no, what's the word? Progressive couples. I'm very proud. They were up visiting me. They're from Nova Scotia. They were one of the first progressive couples in Nova Scotia. Because they're married, you see. I'm very proud. You see, that wasn't an option when I was a girl. We didn't have that option. You waited for some boy to ask you to dance at the community hall and then you pretty much had your whole life mapped out for you after that point. I'm not saying my daughter has it easier than that . . . but that wasn't even an option when I was a girl.

And so I was in the car, and my daughter was in the car and Lisa, her wife, was driving. Out into the middle of nowhere looking for this German food hall. And, after a while, we'd been driving for a long time, and it didn't seem like we were getting anywhere at all, except lost.

Then, we started driving past a certain series of fields. And the birds in these fields! Crows. Each field we passed had these murders in them. Large groups of them. And as we went along, passing these fields, I swear, my Lord, each field we passed the crows kept getting bigger. Bigger and bigger, each field we passed. By the time we had passed five or so fields, the crows, I swear were so big they could rival an eagle, my Lord. They kept getting bigger and bigger, and we kept driving further and further out into the middle of nowhere . . .

Gave me the creeps.

There's not a lot of me left, my Lord. I'm so little. But these birds started giving me the creeps, because I felt like we were somehow getting lost, even though we knew where we were going. Those Germans, they just live so far out there. And I'm so little. I got the goosebumps, and there's not very much of me so when I get the goosebumps, I get the shivers, too, and I almost freeze to death when that happens. I get cold, I swear. I almost froze to death I got so spooked.

Those crows are certainly well fed.

I don't know why those Germans have to live all the way out in the middle of nowhere.

But the food hall was full! We had to park on the road because their parking lot was full!

And we had black forest cake for dessert. It was some good.

When Lisa drove us back home here to Sussex, it was already dark out. So I couldn't have seen those crows again if I had wanted to. And you'd think that'd put me at ease, except it didn't, because I knew those big things were still out there somewhere. In the dark.

Black feathers fading into the night. Sticking their ugly beaks into garbage and road-kill corpses.

Maybe they sleep.

I don't dislike crows. But, my Lord, they shouldn't ever be allowed to get so big as eagles.

It's just not natural.

2.

EVAN, 43 (SAINT JOHN, NB)

I had five dollars left to my name. Five entire dollars. But we needed milk. So I went down to the fuckin' convenience store, and I bought some fuckin' milk. And the fuckin' milk cost two dollars and sixty-five fuckin' cents.

Being unemployed ain't fuckin' easy. It ain't fuckin' easy. All those assholes with jobs who go around talkin' like fuckin' job narcs. "Oh, that guy's drawin' EI? How come he's drawin' fuckin' EI, and I gotta work for a living? He doesn't deserve EI. What's he doin'? Sitting on his ass at home and getting' paid for it from the taxes they take out of me, and I gotta work?" Fuckin' job narcs. Pretty much everybody. EI don't get you much. It's enough to get by but barely, FYI. If you still wanna live, you gotta look for under-the-table stuff to supplement the fuckin' EI. Everyone knows that. And those fuckin' job narcs will fuckin' tattle on you they see you working and drawing EI so watch out for them. Except "them" are everybody. So watch out for everybody, brother.

Watch out for everybody.

Had five bucks to my name. Milk costs two fuckin' sixty-five, and I'm walking home with the milk. Didn't take it in a bag because bags are plastic, and I give a shit about the environment so I'm just holding the carton in my hand. Got my left hand holding the carton. Swinging back and forth because of my natural fuckin' gait.

Meanwhile on the home front, Lyla's losing her sweet fuckin' shit because we're payin' rent but just barely. Never mind the fuckin' phone bill, which is about to hit us. Never mind the power bill. Never mind the MasterCard, student loan, gym membership dues.

Five bucks to my name, and the milk is swinging in my hand because of my natural gait.

And I don't know what I was thinking because the carton, it was a bit wet with moisture from being in the shitty convenience store fridge.

I dropped the fuckin' milk. More like, it flew right out of my fuckin' hand.

Because of my natural gait.

Of course, it explodes on the sidewalk in front of me.

Of course, it fuckin' explodes.

Like everything I ever had fuckin' explodes.

Or I drop it. Or some bullshit.

Stood there for a full minute just staring it. The carton. Exploded. On the sidewalk. Big white puddle.

Big white fuckin' mess.

Turn around walk back to the convenience store. I walk in fast. Stride briskly to the shitty glass door fridge in the back. Grab another milk carton wet with condensation. Get up to the counter put the change left in my pocket down on the counter quick and make to, like, walk out of the place before the guy can count it. "Whoa, whoa, whoa!" He says. The fuckin' . . . kid. "Whoa, whoa, whoa!" He says it just like that. "That's not enough."

And I stop, and I turn, and I look at him. Kid's like maybe nineteen years old. And he has glasses. Skinny as hell. Like a toothpick. But I can see it in his eyes. I can see it. In his . . . eyes. He doesn't know about under-the-table life stuff yet. He's too young. He can't see the complexities of . . . a situation like this. He can't . . .

And I feel the bile rising in my throat. I can feel the hate and violence inside me, the fear and hate and violence in my body about to come out, and so I open my mouth—

And I start begging the kid. I start crying, sorta, weeping, almost. I address the kid as sir, even though I must be fifteen years older than him.

"Oh, sir, I'm really sorry. But please let me have the milk. I dropped the last carton on the street by accident, and Lyla really needs her milk for her cereal, and I don't know what I'm gonna do!

I dunno what I'm going to do, sir! Please, sir! Please just . . . just let me have the milk, sir. I won't bother you ever again, I promise, I promise—"

I'm losing it, right? In front of this kid. He didn't know what hit him. He was just kind of stunned. Staring at me. So I turned and ran.

I ran out of the store and down the street, and I kept running until I found this set of bushes, and I crawled in under them, and I hid. I hid in some bushes. And I couldn't stop crying. I cried and I cried for about twenty minutes.

Like I was ten years old or something. I was nearly fuckin' hyperventilatin' from it.

So when I got home, I told Lyla I was through being in a relationship with her. Then I got to watch her cry for a while.

Made me feel better.

3.

MURRAY, 64 (BLACKS HARBOUR, NB)

Wife an' I are from Maine. Ayuh. We go on vacation every year in Canada. Usually out west. We scoot up through Montreal and head west. But this year we figured we'd try the Maritimes for a change. Ayuh. Somethin' different for a change. It gets awful flat out west anyway, before you hit the Rockies. I seen enough prairie dogs and never-ending horizon, that's for sure.

We don't like it places where it gets too hot. Althea, she never wants to go to Florida. We tried goin' south once. Got as far as New York and even New York was too hot for us. It's hot in New York. You might not believe but it's hot in New York. Ayuh. Too hot for the two of us. We like things cooler than that. And Althea, she got the hot flashes, ayuh, no goin' south now, that's for certain. Not with the hot flashes.

We heard Grand Manan was real pretty in the summer, that's why we came. I'm retired. Just retired. Ayuh. Had a garage in Freeport. We did a lot of business. A lot of tourists go to Freeport for L.L. Bean and all the shopping and everything. Nice thing about being a mechanic in a tourist town . . . ya get to work on a lot of different vehicles. Ayuh. I've worked on every make and model you can imagine. Never a Torino, though. Always wanted to get under a Torino, never got to do that, though. Kind of odd, now that I think about that. Ayuh.

There's apparently whales, you can see on the way over sometimes, if you're lucky. On the crossing to the island. I think they're humpback whales. Not one hundred percent on that, but I think so, anyways. We've seen whales before, out in British Columbia, but those were orcas. Not humpbacks. Orcas are pretty enough, though. Ayuh.

Ayuh, apparently they make good dulse over there too in Grand Manan. Ayuh. Good dulse. You ever tried dulse? It's good. Salty. Yummy. Ayuh. It's seaweed. They take seaweed off the rocks. They collect the stuff. Then they take it and they dry it out and then they sell it like that. And you can get it, buy it softer or crispy. I like the crispy stuff, myself. The crispy dulse. Ayuh.

People will eat anything, I guess. I love the stuff. It's just seaweed. Ayuh.

A few years ago, Althea she got me to go vegetarian with her. Let me tell you, I think she may have saved my life. I feel a lot better now. We don't eat anything except vegetables and fish. And I don't miss being a carnivore one bit. Let me tell you. Ayuh. Maybe bacon. Bacon was pretty good, but did you know they've come up with this kind of dulse that tastes exactly like bacon? So if you're a vegetarian and you miss the flavour of bacon, you can get that flavour but still stay a vegetarian. It was big news, last year. Last year or the year before. It was on all the news stations. Ayuh.

The stuff over in Grand Manan, it's not the bacon-flavoured stuff. But it's still good. Better than most of the dulse you'll ever try. Best in the world, some say. Ayuh.

Quite the scenery in Grand Manan, apparently, but I'm lookin' forward to the dulse. Ayuh.

What were we talkin' about again?

Althea. Whales. Dulse.

So that ferry'll be here in another hour.

Apparently it's free to take the ferry over. Free to get over to the island, but they charge ya if you wanna come back.

Somethin' like forty bucks. To come back. But to get onto the island, it's free.

Ayuh.

Waitin' for a boat.

Ayuh.

Kind of exciting, isn't it?

Ayuh.

Ayuh.

Kind of exciting.

4.

KIT, 32 (CASTALIA, NB)

There aren't too many people trying to get on a lobster boat, I mean, that aren't from the island here. If you live here, yeah, it's what you do. Unless you go to college, university, somethin'.

It can be fun. There are moments. Like right now, you see that pink glow of the sun that's about to rise over the horizon there? Smoking a doob. Boys in the back fixin' the bait, but I get to take us out. This part is almost the best part. The best part is when you get back inta port, of course. But this part, the takin'-us-out part, that's the second-best part.

The rest of the day's just a haul. It's just business. Takin' up traps. Collectin' your interest. Every lobster a few more bucks.

So you took your Gravol, I hope. If this is your first time out on one of these. Hopefully you brought extra; that stuff wears off after a few hours. You gotta keep poppin' them if you got land legs.

Not everyone does that well, where we're goin'. The grey zone. They call it the grey zone because it's international waters. Different rules apply. That's why we can set our traps there right now.

I got a good head for it. My dad has a boat, but he doesn't have the head for it that I do, and I could tell that back when I was a kid. But my dad's a good businessman. Natural at the social aspect of it all. See, I wasn't. Good at the business part of it. That's why I went to university to get my business degree. And when I got that, I came back . . . not to go back workin' on his boat, but to start up my own. Now, I got Magnus and Harold here with me . . . and their take-home is better than the guys on my dad's crew because I know how to read lobster.

You can't think about the water, when you're after lobster, right? Lobster, they're … they travel like a herd … like a ground animal, you know? They're stampeding across the geography of the ocean floor; they're not swimming around like fish. That's why you gotta think about geography when you're a lobster fisherman. You gotta think about the landscape. Under the water. Forget about the water itself and think about the landscape underneath it.

So out here, where we got our traps … under the water … the lobster, they're gonna be heading in this direction, right? As per their regular migration. And I know that there are mountains under the water here and here. So those lobster … the herd of lobster, naturally they're gonna end up passing through the valley between those two mountains. Because they're going in that direction and there's these two mountains … I mean … part of it is common sense, right? So we place our traps in the bottleneck of the valley and when we pull them up … our traps are pretty consistently full. Because we put them down in the high-traffic areas … or what I know will become the high-traffic areas because I'm paying attention to the geography and not the water.

You wanna testament to my methods you go back and ask Magnus and Harold. Harold just bought a new pickup. Magnus just bought a new Xbox, I guess … he's a fuckin' nerd.

You're lucky because today's so calm. I see you turning green now, because that Gravol's wearing off, but take my word for it … this is as good as it gets.

The other day, the water was rough. And we were pushin' it. Trying to get as much done as possible. Sometimes we get like that. Sometimes we're fuckin' fearless out here. It's stupid.

We were out here in the grey zone, and it started getting dark. And dark is … well … goes from clear to dark real quick and when it's dark out here it's fuckin' dark. Gotta rely on the equipment, basically. That's all you got, you know.

There was this flash of light. Kind of pulsing flash of light that started up over the water. Couldn't have been more than a kilometre away from us. And it was … not something any of us had ever seen before, you know? Harold's got video of it on his cellphone.

This weird purple, kind of like this oval throbbing sphere of light . . .
less than a kilometre away, really. And at first we thought it must
have been the Americans with some kind of new kind of spotlight
or beacon or something. But then the light started moving. And
it seemed to be coming straight at us. This purple, glowing throb.
And it kept get bigger and bigger. I hollered at Magnus to get the
seal rifle from below and he went down to get it . . . and this light
it kept getting bigger and bigger . . . like it was coming straight at
us and then . . . it was just gone. I mean, it just stopped being. And
me and Harold were just staring into the dark again. Magnus came
back up with the seal rifle, but I mean . . . the light was gone, right?

And my thoughts are it must have been the Americans somehow. Like, maybe not fishermen. Maybe the military. Some kind
of American military technology, maybe they were trying out some
new kind of drone or something. Because I never seen anything like
it before, and I been out on the water my entire life.

I told my dad about it but he thinks I'm making it up, trying
to trick him somehow or give him the willies. He's kind of never
trusted me since I started having my own boat. But that's his shit.
That has nothing to do with me.

That's the thing, right? I smoke weed. I know I smoke weed. But
I smoke weed because I like weed. I know myself. And I'm smart. I
get what's going on around me. And I know geography. And I know
business. And I know fishing. I'm doing what I'm supposed to be
doing, you know? But what we saw the other night . . . that had no
place in any of it. What we saw the other night . . . that was something that didn't belong. It was real. But it didn't belong. I can't
figure it out.

Hasn't affected our luck with the lobster. Fuck, we had a great
haul on Wednesday.

Doesn't incline me to stay out here any longer than we have to
anymore, either.

5.

VALERIE, 45 (ST. GEORGE, NB)

Not that much here, is there? Is that what you're thinking? You are one hard-up looking kid, anyone ever tell you that? When was the last time you showered? Look at you, turning beet red. Embarrassed. So you're coming here all the way from Halifax. And you're recording people. Like some kind of hobby journalist. One of those journalists taking a year off from all your rag-azine writing to focus on one of those feel-good type of books you've always wanted to write. One of those books you read where people talk about their problems, and you collect them all and then the people reading the book they see all of these other people with problems just like theirs and all of a sudden they don't feel so alone because, "Holy shit, check out all of these people with problems just like mine." One of those books that don't ever work. Not unless the person reading it is a wingnut in the first place.

That's what you're up to, isn't it?

Name's Valerie Greene. I'm forty-five. I'm a pizzeria worker here in the unbelievably beautiful St. George, New Brunswick. Isn't it beautiful here? It's so beautiful here. Gag me with a fork it's so beautiful here. Look at the sea! Look at the water! Look at the trees!

Water and trees and gag me with a fork.

I'm here because I can't be anywhere else. Where the heck else would I go? Saint John? The place stinks. Worse than you, even. Hold up, now. Is that a smirk? You smirkin' at me?

You're all gumballs and rose petals because you're on the road. Some kind of great adventure. But let me tell you, the adventure you're on? It's all in your head. It's not real. It's not even an adventure. You're just some kid scruffing it the hard way, on foot, across a destitute region of a penniless province full of people with good intentions and zero common sense.

Everyone should move out west. We should all head west.

I should move out west, right? Except I'd get out there and have to work at some other shitty pizzeria and, instead of dealing with New Brunswickers, I'd be dealing with Albertans who are even bigger dinks than New Brunswickers and, even though I'd be making more money, sure, everything costs more out there so it all evens out, so what's the big effing deal?

I wouldn't get along with anyone out there. I mean, I don't get along with anybody here, but at least the people here are kind enough to put up with me.

I used to be kind.

But, and I'm not going to get into the why about that, that part of me died when I was a little kid.

Everything you see around you? That's all there really is. Any adventure you perceive exists in your head and in your head, only.

And everywhere else, it's the same thing, too. Every day. Everywhere.

Nothing changes, and this is it.

All you can do is take stock. Don't invest. Just take stock. Don't build.

Rinse and repeat this about ten gazillion times, and you might get lucky and find yourself dead of natural causes.

If not, there's always the lovely cancer. The charm of dementia. There's always the Parkinson's.

My husband suffered.

When I was a kid, my parents suffered.

I'm not going to get into all of that.

Not for your hopeful little book you're writing, anyway.

You badgered me with your flattery. This is fitting punishment for you.

The road ahead of you is nothing but a road.

Asphalt and tar. Black Death.

Your adventure will never exist.

6.

KATHLEEN, 47 (ST. STEPHEN, NB)

That's me for yuh. In a nutshell. I'm a nutcase. Nutcase in a nutshell. I keep buying these stupid tickets. I keep hopin' God will send me a winner, but he never does. He throws Kathleen to the wilderness, as per usual. I must have bought over a thousand lotto tickets in my lifetime. I bought so many lotto tickets that, by now, I'd probably be a millionaire if I'd had just taken the money I spent on all of those tickets and invested it. I could probably be living off the interest of all that money I would have saved, or made off investing it.

But I keep buyin' them. I keep doing it. And I know, I know. I know I'm doin' it to myself. I know I'm keeping myself in the hole like this. I know better, but I keep doin' it, and I know that.

At least I know that about myself, right?

I even quit smoking a few years back. I quit smoking, and I haven't been a drinker since my youth . . . could quit drinking and even smoking, but I continue to buy these stupid lotto tickets. Keep waiting for the big one. Keep waiting for that big thing that's gonna swoop down and pick me up like the rapture.

I think that maybe I secretly but not so secretly hate my life. Or something like that. There's gotta be a reason.

If I ever won the lottery, I know exactly what I'd do with it, too. The money. I wouldn't give it to charity. I wouldn't give half of it to my family or anything like that. I'd put it right into the bank and live off the interest. I wouldn't be miserly, though. If anyone ever asked me for a hundred dollars here or there, I'd give it to them. But you won't catch me throwing it away.

I been living hand to mouth too long now. If I ever win the stupid thing, I won't be giving it all away. Maybe that sounds rude or mean. But I'm telling you . . . I'm not a rude or mean person. I just been in need of money for so long, I don't plan on screwing myself over if I can ever get myself outta this situation, you hear me?

I wouldn't buy a fancy car. I wouldn't buy fancy clothes. I'd pay my debts, and I'd be here for people if they needed me and that is it.

I'd be a rock for people. If someone needed something, they could come to me and I'd help them. And that'd be it.

I'd be something solid in this ever-shifting world.

And I'd get rid of my cellphone and offa the Facebook, too, because, really, who needs any of that foolishness when you're good enough on your own?

I'd keep using email and talking to people on the street but that would be it.

I wouldn't buy a new car, but I'd fix up my Corolla. I'd get all the parts on it replaced and make sure that it'd last forever. Right now, the underpanels have started to rust, and I might have to get rid of it. But I don't want to get rid of it. It's always been a good car. Served me well. I don't have the money to get the bodywork done on 'er, but I don't want to get rid of her, either. Even though she'll never pass inspection as is.

So if I win the lotto this week, I'll make sure to fix 'er up. My Corolla.

I think that's what's more alluring than anything else, you hear me?

About the lotto.

It isn't the money part about the lotto that everyone wants. It's the idea that life will just . . . all of a sudden, you win the lotto . . . life becomes solid. You got nothing to worry about. You don't have to worry about your car fallin' apart. About people you care about runnin' into debt or bankruptcy or gettin' sick or senile or . . .

Everyone thinks that winning the lotto is gonna turn them into rocks.

They'd be somethin' solid in this ever-shiftin' world.

Time would just wash over us like stones in a brook. We wouldn't move. We wouldn't break down.

We'd just smooth out.

And stay put.

Here in St. Stephen.

SEPTEMBER

LOWELL (LOON BAY, NB)

I don't know if you can hear that or not. I'm not sure if the recorder is going to pick it up. Do you hear it?

I mean, there's crickets, there. For sure. The occasional loon.

The crickets or the cicadas . . . they're singing. I think they're singing. I'm not sure why. But I can hear them. And their song, it changes octaves every once and a while.

They're singing along in this high pitch, and then, after a minute or so, they switch to this lower pitch. A different note, or chord. High, then low. Can you hear it?

Why do they keep switching it up? Why does the song keep changing, and how come it changes for all of them? All at the same time? Like they're all linked or something.

My fire is dying. I'm going to have to look around for more wood.

I'm the only person at this campground right now. It's pitch black right now, except for the stars and my campfire. There are a ton of stars, though.

The sound around me is just so immense. Like it's everywhere. Everything.

It's not the ocean . . . but . . . well, it's hard to describe. In a good way.

I'm trying to look it up on my cellphone, and the word the Internet is giving me is "tremolo." Tremolo. Such a cool word. Two notes at different pitches that produce an overtone. Give and take. I wish I knew more about how music worked. Tremolo.

Okay, I'm going to go get some wood now. I'll leave the recorder on so that maybe it will get this on tape.

Because it is beautiful. It's not the ocean, but it is beautiful.

Tremolo.

1.

SAMUEL, 42 (MCADAM, NB)

We get a lot of groups comin' through, five or six per week, wantin'
to run the St. Croix. So they give us the keys to their vehicles, we
help them put in up here at Vanceboro, and then me and my wife
Kayleigh, we run their vehicles downstream via this gravel road back
to Loon Bay. Takes about twenty minutes to drive there, and it can
be a two-day paddle by canoe. You can do the route in one day; it's
just not very relaxing if you do it that way. Most people put in at the
Vanceboro train bridge and canoe to Little Falls with a few beers in
their coolers, camp on either the American or Canadian side and
then the next morning, they finish their run the rest of the way.

Quieter this summer than most. And now that it's really winding
down, now that we've passed the Labour Day weekend . . .

I mean, there isn't a whole hell of a lot to do here. So you got
some time on your hands, is what I'm sayin'.

And because the river traffic is down . . . well, I'm less busy than
I normally am, and . . . even when the river traffic is high, it still
gets quiet around here at night, so you kind of notice things, when
something out of the ordinary happens.

My son, he's twelve now. He knows better than to pull any horseshit now, but last year, he was still in that hard-to-control phase
of his life. Or he kept actin' like he was hard to control. We kept
sitting around here waiting to see what kind of horseshit he'd get
himself into next.

Well, last year, last spring, he decided to cross the Vanceboro
train bridge. Because no one's lookin', right? And I mean, if you
walked up to it, the Vanceboro train bridge, that's what you'd think,

if you were a kid. "No one's lookin.'" And so, my son, he figured he'd run across the thing. Because the tracks are derelict. There's no trains anymore. And the bridge itself, I mean, looks so derelict . . .

Funny thing about that bridge. They'll let high schoolers swim under the thing, and attach their tow ropes so they can surf the rapids, the current's that strong there . . . but if you try crossin' the thing . . . no sir.

So my son, thinkin' no one's watchin', he starts walking across the thing . . . they had a helicopter on him before he could touch the other side. Helicopter came outta nowhere.

And I've crossed the border to Vanceboro here a bunch of times. And the guards at the border . . . I don't know if they hire them from away or what, but they always seem to have Texan accents, and they're always wearing sunglasses . . . not the friendliest, is what I'm trying to say. Good at their job, but not the friendliest.

My son almost got arrested. They did take him into custody. My eleven-year-old. We had to get the RCMPs to negotiate him free. I don't even know how they managed to do it. And the Americans, they were pissed. Right off. Ever since the 9/11 stuff . . . you don't walk across the Vanceboro bridge. Not as a kid, not as no one.

I mean, my son's settled down since. We got him a cat. One of those leopard-lookin' ones. He's taken right to it. Calls the thing "Morris."

So what's my point, right?

See, it's quiet around here now. It's quiet out here normally, but right now it's even quieter because of the lack of traffic on the river, and maybe that's why I've noticed.

Started last week. In the middle of the night. All of these sirens started going off in the middle of the night out by the bridge. And I mean, we can see the thing from our house. The Americans, they had their sirens goin' and the helicopter out with the spotlight, and I could see the agents, and I could hear the dogs . . . Monday of last week. Around two or three in the morning. Dead of night, right?

Well, let me tell you this. There has been two nights since where the exact same damn thing has happened. The sirens. The helicopter. The searchlights. The men. The dogs. Somethin' has got those border agents all riled up. Riled up to the point where they're all hands on deck in the middle of the night.

I asked Sergeant Harris about it. Sergeant Harris is the resident . . . what would you call him? Commanding officer of the local RCMP detachment. I told him about it. How I seen the border patrol out there, doing this stuff. Three times so far. Dead of night. He told me they're probably just on the lookout for smugglers.

And let me tell you this. People been smuggling shit across this river since the 1800s, since forever. And even after 9/11, I never seen the border guard this riled up. Not ever.

And I told that to Sergeant Harris as well. And he just shrugged it off. And that's bullshit, too.

The RCMP are a great many things, but uninformed ain't one of them.

He shrugged off what I was sayin', because he knew something about it. Because the RCMP here have many a time worked with those guys at the border patrol. And if the border patrol is riled, the RCMP know somethin' about it, at least.

Queer.

We picked up a family, yesterday. Something had shaken them. Halfway along their run. When they camped overnight at Little Falls. On the American side. And they were Canadians and shouldn't have been camping on the American side, so they couldn't approach any authority about it. Now, the parents weren't interested in telling me anything about it, but you could just tell something had happened. And the only reason I came to know anything at all about it was because their little girl, she was about ten, she said something that made me kind of wonder.

"We saw eyes in the dark."

That's what she said.

And she could have been talkin' about anything. But she said it to me. Like she was reporting it. Like I was the RCMP and not just a part-time vehicle caddy.

So very damn queer.

What's getting everyone so riled up, do you suppose?

2.

STACY, 21 (FREDERICTON, NB)

Hi! Hello. Hello! I'm Stacy! And this guy, Lowell, Lowell is the bomb, mutherfuckers! He's the fuckin' . . . absolutely the fuckin' bomb! Just bump and throw it, just bump and throw that shit, kay? That's my new catchphrase. Just bump and throw that shit! Hey! Hey! You know what? Lowell is so cool! Lowell is a cool mutherfuckin' playah! He's a playah bitches!

I am too drunk for this. What are we even . . . what are we even doing this for?

I meant, hello! I'm Stacy! I'm Lowell's buddy's roommate . . . JP! But JP's at work right now. He doesn't get off until three a.m. There was this other guy, this security guard who went missing on his shift, just up and vanished. They even brought in the cops to try and figure out where he went . . . but yeah, so they had to fill in the shifts . . . but nobody knows where this guy went or what the fuck is up with him disappearing . . . and so JP has to cover all of these extra shifts and . . .

But Lowell is staying at my place for the night here in Fredericton until he can find himself a real job. No, wait. I meant, he's travelling. He's travelling. He's only staying with me until he decides to take the fuck off! Take it up and out of F-town! YOLO! Bump and throw that shit!

No, but seriously, I can't blame you. Not. One. Little. Bit. Go. Leave New Brunswick. There is no money here. Seriously. There is no fucking money here. There is no money here. But you just gotta bump and throw that shit. You just gotta bump and . . . but seriously, get the fuck out of here. Because there's no money. There is literally no money. Go. Go. Go. You gotta . . . just . . . go. Man.

My brother is working in a camp. In Alberta. Fort McMurray. The camp's outside of Fort McMurray, like out in the tundra somewhere. But he has an apartment in Fort McMurray, where he can save money and go to the gym and do all the cocaine he wants. That's where you should be. That is the place, man. Fort Mac! Yolo!

I have a boyfriend. I just want you to know that. Because I have a boyfriend. And his name is . . . fuck. What's his name again? Sarah? Sarah! Sarah! Come in here! I want you to tell me what my boyfriend's name is again! C'mon! Pleeeeeeaaaaase! Sarah! Sarah! Bitch.

The "J" stands for Jacob. Or Jeremy. Or Jason. Jack. I don't know what the "P" stands for. Poutine? Parachute?

Don't worry. Just don't worry about it. JP will be back. He's filling in for that guy who went missing right now, but he will be back.

I like your hair. It smells like a tree.

Doesn't it seem, like, so fuckin' weird to you how this town is? Like, everyone in this town knows everyone in this town. And this town isn't even supposed to be a town. It's supposed to be a city. Can you pass me the Jägermeister?

When a place is small like this. But it's got like, these big aspirations? Like, how this place wants to be a city, even though it's so small it might as well be a town? So everyone is always all up in everybody's grill. Seriously. That's F-town for ya. It's worse than a *Real Housewives* episode. And there's so many bitches. So many bitches. And they're always all up in your grill, you copy? Like Sarah. YOU BITCH! SARAH! YOU'RE SUCH A BITCH! But you just gotta bump and throw that shit. Bump and throw that shit to the wind. Yolo!

You might be cute.

You might have a really good soul. I might be able to tell.

But are you drunk right now? That's the important question.

If my boyfriend comes back and sees you recording me, he might get pissed. He gets jealous. Once he beat up a guy because he was just talking to me. Downtown. We were waiting to get a slice of pizza and this nice guy came up and started just talking to me, and my boyfriend and his buddies ripped off their shirts and kicked the living shit out of him. And he didn't do anything to deserve that. He was just talking to me about his real estate job. He was innocent.

I'm innocent, too.

If I kiss you, do you promise not to tell? Like anyone.

I won't tell. I won't even tell that bitch Sarah and she's, like, seriously, my best friend since birth.

You smell like pine cones. Or baby wombats. You smell like you might be cute.

3.

JP, 22 (FREDERICTON, NB)

Naw, boy. I'm good. I'm ready for this. Roll the tape. Roll it. Are we rolling?

What do you think of my moustache? Pretty slick, eh? Security guard moustache. Not hipster. Legit. Sometimes, when I'm drinking coffee, it absorbs some of the coffee when I drink it, and I have to suck the coffee out of it afterwards.

Stacy told you about Ian, eh? The guard who went missing? My boss thinks he just quit. Except I know Ian. So it's kind of strange to me. It gets spooky in that place, at night. I've started carrying a baton around with me. Even though if I saw anything, I'd probably just take off running. Like an actual criminal or anything? I mean, they're just paying me minimum wage. If a thief has a knife on him? Not worth it. I don't even care about the paintings in that place. But Ian liked security. It was his thing. He was one of those types. He had an awesome moustache. Handlebars. To make him look more like a cop. Big and bushy, and he even had the moustache fangs, eh? So what happened?

But I guess that's not the big news. There's something else I wanna tell you about. Since you're in town, out of the blue and everything.

The big news is that I'm in a relationship, with a girl and she's amazing. She is like, the best. I met her at the bar one block over from here. Her name is Isa, and she is the most amazing woman I have ever met in my life, and she is mine, and I am in this great place with her right now, and we are getting married in May of next year. She even likes my moustache.

There's pumpkin in this coffee. Yes, it's pumpkin. Did you get the same coffee as me? I asked for a dark roast.

I have been noticing more of the details of life since I've met Isa.

Such a beautiful day. The air. You can feel it in the air, it's starting to turn. It's not too hot anymore . . . you can feel that chill underneath it. That fall air. Fall air has this bite to it that . . . you know? You can feel it comin' on now. Time to retire those flip-flops. Time to wear real shoes again. Dust off the sweaters. Bring the wool back into circulation.

Fredericton in the summer, it's too hot. In the fall, it's better. Better to be in Saint John in the summer; they get the breeze from the coast. The Bay of Fundy. But Fredericton is too hot in the summer. That's why I'm so happy for the fall.

I like the cold better than the heat. You can always warm yourself up. It is harder to cool yourself off than it is to warm yourself up.

I still love looking at the ladies. I'm about to get married, but the women . . . I can't stop looking at the women, right? I mean, look at that. Look at her. Who is she, do you think? I don't know.

You won't be here for the wedding, if you are in Toronto. You will be missing out. We are going to have it at her father's farm. Open bar. You would like it. Lots of her friends. Lots of my friends. Lots of ladies. Jane's coming down for it. From Montreal. You gonna visit her on your way through Quebec? It's been awhile since the three of us have hung out. Fucking Lawrencetown, man! Surfing! She taught us all how to surf.

Remember that time she saved your life?

She keeps checking in on me. She called the other day. To confirm she's coming to the wedding. Jane's cool, right? You always thought she was cool, right? You should email her.

If you can't make the wedding, we need to stay in touch. Too many of my friends . . . they just seem to run off. Disappear. Like Connor in Saskatchewan. But we need to stay connected to one another. We're social animals. It is not good for us to . . . remain distant. It's not our nature. Our nature is . . . like an orchestra. We need to reverberate against each other. We need to party, to have fun. We need proximity. We need to smell each other's teeth. Feel each other's heat. Nothing brings you back into contact with life more than realizing you are near someone, and that that person is hot. You get me? If you were European, you would get me. New Brunswickers are so cold. They're so distant and conservative.

After I marry Isa, we're going to Honduras for our honeymoon. And we will drink tequila and champagne from coconuts and go drunk snorkelling. My father, he travelled the world when he was young. He went to Australia, to the Great Barrier Reef, and when he was there, he rode a whale shark. He grabbed onto its fin and away he went. But my adventures shall exceed his.

I love it here. The fall is fantastic. I have not worn this sweater for six months.

What do you think of her? Over in the corner. The one in the jean jacket with the glasses. I could introduce you to her. I know her from university. She is friendly.

Do you know, when we speak? I feel like now, as we talk, as I talk to you . . . I'll never see you again after today. Do you feel that? Do you? I feel desperate talking to you. Like I am losing you. Society is like an ecosystem, you know? We gotta preserve it.

I want you come back here for the wedding. I want you and Jane back for the wedding. May of next year. Connor, too, if I ever manage to reach him. Saskatchewan's a big place.

You could just stay here. You could crash on my couch a couple weeks until you found a job. An apartment. Stacy wouldn't mind. Stay here and hang out in F-town with me and help me plan the wedding. You could be my best man. But you would have to grow a moustache so that we would match in the photos. Not to pressure you or anything.

But where are you going, Lowell? I mean, really. Do you know? Turn off the recorder and tell me the truth.

4.

LILY, 56 (MEDUCTIC, NB)

The closest town to here is Woodstock, that's a ten-minute drive north. So you only had enough money to get you here, eh? You're going to need money to get to Tofino, of all places. I know a few people in Jacksonville . . . it's harvest season, so they might be able to use an extra hand. Not sure if they can set you up with enough to get to Tofino or not. Depends on how much work you do for 'em, I guess.

Maybe Wade could help you. Wade McLeod. He's got a potato farm . . . he might need some help. Only place here in Meductic is the cymbal factory, and they aren't hiring right now. It's a good place to work, but I don't think they need anyone at the moment. Wade might need someone, though. You ever worked on a farm before?

Everything up here . . . it's not what you know, but who you know. I mean, it's a bit what you know. But, more than anything, it's who you know. You know? And I'm related, I guess you could say, to Wade. We're third cousins. Don't ask me what that means, my mother explained it to me years ago when she was still alive.

It's enough, though, to ask him if he's got work so, yes, I'll do that.

What are you going to Tofino for?

I see Rick Mercer on the television, interviewing people from all walks of life across Canada. Is this what this is? Kind of?

I just get worried, you see. Being recorded. It's like you're taking what I say, and well, I guess if you write a book on it . . . I don't get to edit myself, if you record me, and I don't know where this is goin', is all.

Because, really . . . we're a pretty quiet place.

Overall.

There was a man in here, two days ago. Sort of out of sorts. Raving about weird stuff. Stuff you can't repeat. If I tell you, you can't repeat it, okay? Even if you're recording me. Okay?

Please don't.

Guy said he saw a UFO.

Honest to God. Came right in here. Late at night. We were almost closed. Started raving about it. Some kind of UFO he saw. Drove up, gassed up his car, came inside here, and just was rantin'. For like, five whole minutes. About this UFO he saw.

Then he bought some pepperoni sticks and a couple of Fun Dips, and then he left.

Maybe keep this off the record.

I don't need people sayin' I'm spreading any kind of hysteria or nothing.

UFOs are fake anyway. Guy was probably some kind of psycho.

Usually, I can tell if people are crazy or not. I can get a feel for people. Just by meeting them.

For instance, I wouldn't be offerin' to give Wade McLeod a call if you struck me as such . . . Crazy or whatever.

You seem all right. You need a shower, though. Maybe a haircut. Wade won't care about that, though. How's your back? You got to bend over a lot with that work. Because potatoes grow in the ground, eh? You gotta bend over to get them. I used to help pick potatoes, but my lower vertebrae are all pretty much fused together now, I'm no use to the farmers, anymore.

You'll be all right. I got your cellphone. Maybe he'll call ya.

If I end up sounding weird on the playback, then you erase it, you hear?

So you gonna walk to Woodstock, or are ya gonna keep hitch-hikin'? Hitchhikin's illegal here, but the RCMP here won't give a damn. They won't do anything to ya, or anything. I mean, what could they do? Drive you to the outskirts? We're already on the outskirts. The whole of Meductic is the outskirts.

Welcome to the River Valley, city kid.

5.

NATHAN, 34 (WOODSTOCK, NB)

You know how it gets at night. Well, I mean, you don't know. You don't know, you're new here. But the rest of us, I mean, me, I know. How it gets here at night. The rest of us here on the river road know. How it gets. Here at night. But you're still new so I'll walk you through it.

This whole river valley serves as a flight path for UFOs. Let me be the one to tell you that. They use it as a flight path. Like, the geography. The valley. It's easy to navigate or something. It's a valley, see? So the traffic, the UFOs . . . right through the valley. You get it? It's all about geography.

Weird lights are nothin' new to us. Not to the people who live here. First off, we live outside of the city, so there's no light pollution down here on the river road. You look up at the night sky; you see it for what it is. It's full glory. You see the Milky Way, you see every single star that can be seen by the naked eye. It's that dark here. No light pollution. That's key. So we see everything. And weird lights, well, I mean, what are we talkin' here? Satellites? Space stations? UFOs? This is your front-row seat. This is your VIP ticket. Here, right here. My house. My porch. Right on the water. Right on the bank of the good old Saint John River. Prettiest river in the world by day. By night, the craziest light show you ever did see. You just gotta watch it. And it'll all happen for ya, right in front of your eyes.

So it doesn't surprise me, that lady in Meductic talkin' about that guy who saw the UFOs, not a bit; they use this valley as a flight path. 'Cause of the geography.

But you never see anything but lights, and that's what's weird to me.

What, there's just these aliens or whatnot just hovering around and looking at people?

Here's the question I pose to you. Okay, so you're a shopper. You're in a mall and you're a shopper, and you're just looking at things, right? You're just looking. Just shopping around and just looking. But let me ask you this . . . how many times have you gone shopping, with the intention of just looking . . . how many times— no matter what your intentions are—how many times have you touched?

Am I right?

We touch shit all the time. When we're just looking.

It's a natural . . . thing. It just happens, right?

So we find ourselves on this flight path, right? Us. Humans. UFOs and whatnot zipping by us every night in the darkness.

Just looking, right?

Just looking. No touching.

How bullshit is that?

They're touching something. They're touching someone.

Am I right?

I was scared of ghosts when I was a kid. Now, I'm scared of aliens.

And, I mean, I'm terrified of aliens. I read that Whitley Strieber book, *Communion*, and that did it for me. That sealed the deal. That's the only thing I'm scared of anymore. Besides my ex-wife. And her son. That kid is not right in the head. What he did to that girl at school was not how children should behave.

You know when you smoke a joint, but you leave your front door unlocked when you smoke the joint, you know that feeling?

Two years ago, I went to the Dooryard Arts Festival in the middle of town. And I was drinking and listening to the bands and having a good time, and, when the night ended, I got my buddy to drop me off here at my home, here on the river road. And after he drove off . . . I mean, I was going to go inside the house to have a nightcap and then go to sleep, but the sky was so clear that night. The sky was so clear, and the moon was full and so bright. It was very light out.

Even though it was night. You could see everything. So I sat down beside my house, on the lawn, and I just kind of stared at the river in the night. Everything was so pretty and peaceful, and there was no wind, and everything was calm and the moon was lovely and—

All of a sudden, there was this crazy shrieking that started up. Down near the riverbank. And I didn't know what it was. I assumed it was some animal, but I hightailed it into the house because I didn't know. I didn't know what it was. That was after midnight. I was by myself.

I'm not a brave man, either. I'm more of a . . . well . . . what you would call a reader. I like reading about things the next day in the paper. I don't necessarily want to make contact with things. I keep a safe distance.

But there's all sorts of weird stuff like that happening on the river. Every night.

The river is home to weird stuff.

The geography makes it a flight path. The geography does.

You want another beer? I got more than enough.

You wanna smoke a joint?

6.

EMMA, 47 (WATERVILLE, NB)

Nobody has really asked to talk to me about this, which seems really odd to me. I mean, the RCMP spoke with me. Corporal what's his name. And that little girl working for them now. The ride along. I spoke to both of them. About how he went missing. And they took notes while I was speaking. So I know they got the story. But I haven't heard much about it other than that. Even the other nurses at the hospital aren't talking about it that much, and that's just so odd, you know? I mean, we are busy and everything . . . but a man disappeared. A patient.

It's because, I think, that he was a gomer. You know what a gomer is? A gomer is . . . well . . . they're what the doctors call . . . patients . . . that are just taking up space. They're not going to get cured. They're basically . . . well . . . vegetables.

Which is even more odd. Because this guy, Lyle, Lyle Farrell, and he's actually related to our neighbour through his mother's side. Lyle Farrell. Lyle wasn't able to move himself around, if you know what I mean. He needed help. Getting around. If he needed to use the bathroom, things like that.

He had cancer, and he was terminal. He couldn't move, I guess, is my point. Not without help.

And so I took him in for supper that night. Turkey and peas. He likes peas. And I fed him. And he seemed to be in good spirits. He didn't speak or anything like that, but I think at one point I was telling him a joke, and I think he almost chuckled at the joke. And he ate most of his food. He ate all of his peas because he just loves peas.

I cleaned him up and took his tray out of the room with me. And nothing struck me as odd then.

But when I came back two hours later he wasn't there anymore. Lyle. Lyle was gone. His bed was still warm, but Lyle was gone.

And he couldn't have gotten far on his own. He could barely move. You needed to help him just to get him on his feet. There's just no way he could have walked out of that room fast enough that no one would have noticed. Someone would have seen him. It would have taken him a half an hour just to get to the stairwell. I mean, he couldn't move on his own.

Someone must have taken him.

I told the RCMP that. But they haven't called me since. I don't know what they're doing to follow up on it. And no one at work is talking about it, either. I brought it up the other night to the supervisor. I brought it up casually, just in passing. She changed the subject on me. She wasn't interested in talking about it. Or she didn't want to talk about it, obviously. I don't know if it's because it's an embarrassing situation for the hospital or what. But we lost a patient. I was the last person to see him alive. And I've maybe had three people talk to me about it since. That's odd, isn't it?

They took him right out from under our noses. There's no way into that ward without passing the reception desk. Anyone going in to get him would have had to pass the desk twice. And they would have had to be carrying him, because Lyle wasn't able to move very fast himself.

And we're on the fourth floor, so it's not like he got out through the window.

I've never lost a patient before. I may have forgotten which room one is in from time to time, but I've never flat out lost one, never to be seen again.

To have people not react to something like this . . . it's sad, isn't it? These old people are just withering away, and no one cares. Like people just can't wait to be rid of them. It's sad. It really is sad.

People don't just disappear. Even if they're terminal.

Even if they're gomers, they don't just disappear.

I don't know what I'm supposed to do. I told the RCMP, I gave my report.

I gave my report, and nothing happened.

And Lyle's gone.

Almost like he was never, ever here in the first place.

I live alone. I'm a five-minute drive away from here. On Rosedale Road, running through the woods. What would happen if I went missing? What would happen if someone took me away?

It's been too quiet around here.

Someone's playing games. That's what I think.

Someone's playing games.

OCTOBER

LOWELL (HARTLAND, NB)

I wrote some more stuff about my family of wolves. Whatever it is, whatever it is I'm writing . . . it's starting to take shape, I think.

Cabo was gone. He had taken up Yokka's post in the early morning so that the omega could sleep, and then snuck out before the rest of us woke up. Sertan bit Yokka's front leg hard enough to break hide. I had to get in between them, lick Sertan's lips, and growl before he would release him.

We caught Cabo's scent in the air outside of the farmhouse. We could tell he was moving south. Xyla couldn't understand it. She was still too young. But Sertan knew. Cabo had decided to turn around and face the desperate ones alone. We weren't about to follow him. A week earlier, our pack stood at twenty strong. Now we were down to four.

Cabo had been my youngest. My blood ran hot in his veins. We let him crusade south with a grim acceptance, as we forced ourselves farther into the North.

Last night? At this bed and breakfast I was staying at in Jacksonville . . . had some weird dreams. I woke up with my face down in the pillow, and I freaked out because I was suffocating. Strange way to start the day.

This river valley is gorgeous. All the leaves have turned so just . . . there's so much colour everywhere. Oranges and reds and yellows and purples and browns. Like a painting.

It was good to see JP again in Fredericton. It was good to see him, hear his voice . . . hear him laughing again. When I close my eyes, if I close them really hard, I can almost be there again with him. In

Fredericton, at the tables outside the café. If I close my eyes even harder, I can almost be back in Lawrencetown with him when we were kids. Going surfing with him and Connor and Jane . . . I keep thinking about how no one's heard from Connor in years. It's weird how friends can just go . . . missing. People that mean that much to you.

Today, I'm going to be conducting a little investigation in the town of Hartland. Like the Hardy Boys or Columbo or something. I came across some odd stories when I was at the hospital in Waterville, and I want to check them out, if I can. Patients disappearing from their beds. Some house cats found mutilated in the woods around the parking lot.

Maybe I shouldn't be doing this. Maybe it's not . . . healthy for me to be . . . it's like when someone tells you a house is haunted. And so you go look at the house, even though the last thing anyone really needs to see is a ghost.

1.

MARJORIE, 64 (HARTLAND, NB)

I live in a nice little town, and there's nothin' crazy going on in my life. And that's the way I'd like to keep it. I keep my nose clean, and I don't snoop. I don't gossip. Good. Canadian. Ever. More.

Lyle was half-gone with dementia before the cancer. Scared off most of his friends before anyone figured out it was dementia. He'd been a heavy drinker his whole life, and it doesn't matter if he was a nice enough person when he was nice, because whenever he was on a binge, he was a disgusting man with a temper and . . . because he was an alcoholic, he was basically going off on a binge almost every day of his life and he never saw that as a problem. Which was the problem. Most of his friends left him due to depression. Not Lyle's depression, but their own. Because they'd get so depressed trying to help out their friend when he didn't see anything at all wrong with what he was doing to himself. Nothin' wrong with having a drink or two in the mornin'. And then one after that, and then one after that, and then, "Why not drive to the liquor store for another six-pack because it's a fine afternoon after all, isn't it?" And then driving down there again at eight in the evening because he had finished the six-pack, and he needed another and maybe a quart of rum on top of that to help him sleep. There was the chain-smoking on top of all of that. He looked twenty years older than he ever was. And he was old to begin with. So his friends, his good friends, they'd get on him about this, and then he'd get defensive, because he'd been drinking and wasn't quite sure about himself, and then he'd get scared for himself and that'd make him angry, and the next thing you'd know he'd be stomping around his apartment knocking over chairs and screaming at his friends for being too hard on him, or not under-standing him, which was all a bunch of nonsense. You can only offer someone help so many times. If they keep refusing it . . . well, you wait and see if you get depressed or not. If you liked the person to begin with, and you see them keep doing it to themselves. I mean, eventually you gotta cut ties because it'll break you . . . watching someone you love just go ahead and kill themselves and think that it's okay that they're doing that.

And Emma Hanson has no business insinuating anything happened to him more nefarious than him just running out of there with his dementia and running off into the woods to meet his maker. I mean, my gosh, you hear stories all the time about those night shift nurses, especially the young ones taking naps through their shifts. Lyle had dementia. He'd had it for years, it had progressed, is what I am trying to say. And what is she trying to do to suggest anything outside of that?

Life is a lot more natural than people covering their tracks would have you believe. It's the first defensive tactic of a liar. Deflection. The nurses were napping on shift and a patient escaped. "Oh, well, someone must be playing games." Sure. No one's playing games around here. They should take the German shepherds out around the woods around the hospital is what they should be doing.

Just because a man doesn't have any friends left doesn't mean he has enemies. Other than himself.

And I'm not trying to be hard on those nurses, either. I know they work hard. I know they work long shifts. And I know the province can't afford to pay them right and all of that.

But if they would just admit to the fact that they let him walk out of there . . . then everyone would know, and then there wouldn't be all of this ridiculous gossip going around about Lyle, of all people.

I keep my nose clean. I don't pay attention to gossip. Good. Canadian. Ever. More.

And let's say someone was playing games. I'm certainly not going to tell you about it, of all people. Because if someone is playing games, and I tell you about it, and whoever is playing games finds out I told you anything, well, you're not the police or the RCMP.

What kind of protection would I have if I told you anything? How much protection would I have if I ever told the RCMP? I'm just an old lady. Living by herself because I took care of my health and didn't drink myself stupid and gave myself dementia, prematurely. But what kind of protection could I expect from them, let alone some kind of travelling writer kid?

And you should know better than to be snoopin' around like some kind of Magnum P.I. You don't have any protection. You don't even have anywhere to stay around here. I mean, you need to have your head examined, you ask me.

Lyle's dead in the woods near that hospital, you mark my words.

I keep my nose clean, and so should you. So should Emma Hanson.

Good. Canadian. Evermore.

You should try and get some work and get yourself a place to stay. You should try and get a job rather than whatever it is you call this that you're doing.

That's the last of the tea. When you're finished that I got no more. I gotta go to the store tomorrow to get some more.

This isn't the city. It's dark outside. Man could come into your home at night and kill you, and that'd be it, and no one would know until four or five days later, unless the Mormons came by trying to convert you and they catch whiff of the smell.

Everyone thinks that gossiping and making up stories protects them somehow.

I keep my nose clean.

2.

WADE, 51 (FLORENCEVILLE–BRISTOL, NB)

I'm not sure if we'll be keeping you that long, to be honest. Work'll start winding down pretty quick. Basically, just got a bunch of here-and-there stuff for ya. It's not been that great of a harvest, either. Not been that great of a year, to be completely honest.

Weather just wasn't right. And then all that rain during haying season. I'll be lucky if it doesn't rot half of it halfway through January. I'll have to probably buy some off the neighbours. That'll cut into everything. And a shitty yield. Everything too small. The distributors giving me some horseshit about the potatoes we sent 'em this year. Had to dicker around with the contract because they're worried about the yield next year being like this year. And then the animals on top of everything. The cows, eh? There's something wrong with the cows. Don't know what the hell's up with them.

The milk tastes funny. Can't figure out why. They're acting weird out in the pasture and the milk tastes funny. All of the milk. All of the milk doesn't taste like milk should. And I think it's because they're freaked out about something, but I can't figure out what the hell they have to be freaked out by. I mean, they're cows. It's not like we've stopped looking after them. They have all these goddamned fields to graze. But they're not even grazing like they normally do. Some of them are starting to look lean. I brought the vet out to check them out—that cost an arm and a leg, of course—and he doesn't know what's wrong with them. One of them tried to bite him, he said. Which I figured was horseshit. But he charged me a little heavy, too, and I think that's why. Because he thought one of them tried to bite him, but he thought I thought he was full of horseshit.

It could be just a down year. You have down years sometimes. On the farm. But we had a great year last year, and we were all set to go start of spring and got a head start on everything. And then June came along, and it's just been one thing after the other. All sorts of stupid little things.

Pulled the kid a couple of days from school so's he could lend a hand. The wife nearly took a strip out of my hide for that, when she found out. Which is why I'm bringing you on board. Though I hope I don't have to for very long. No offence. It's just been a heck of a haul, lately.

You don't know how to drive a tractor, and that's a pain in the ass. I suppose I'll have to get Dick to run the tractor, then.

Just be here tomorrow, bright and early, we'll get ya started. However long we keep ya. However long you last.

You're not going to write about that stuff I said about the distributors, are ya? You should probably edit that stuff out. I need the money.

You just find yourself stuck. Most of the time. You know the work that's gotta get done. The work . . . it's stuff you've known since you were a kid. And because you were a kid when you learned the work, you know why it's gotta get done. So there's no putting it off.

I remember seeing my dad when I was a kid and seeing how tired the work made him, and the headaches he used to get. By the end of some days, he'd have migraines so bad he'd skip supper to go lie down on the couch, and you couldn't talk to him, and we'd have to tiptoe around the house if he was like that because any noise we made would set him off. Takes a hell of a lot of stress to make a man get like that.

When I was a kid, I'd see him like this and think to myself, "I'm never gonna get like that. I'm sure as hell never gonna become a farmer."

I thought that right up until grade twelve. Right until I had to choose between working on the farm and going to university.

Now you see those universities struggling with enrolment and all their professors going on strike every other year, and you hear about people with degrees working at Tim Hortons all over the place or driving a cab.

It's like they present ya with two doors, when you're heading outta high school. A door on the left and a door on the right. You know what's behind the first door? Misery and pain. Headaches and sore joints and all the joy life brings. And you know what's behind the second door? Misery and pain. Headaches and sore joints and all the joy life brings.

So you tell me. Which door are you supposed to choose?

Or you could just become a drifter, I guess.

By bright and early, I mean five a.m.

3.

KEITH, 57 (PERTH–ANDOVER, NB)

You will see some of the prettiest sunrises you have ever seen in your entire life on your way home from work. The end of the shift is the best thing about the job. When you're driving in your car on your way home. I know you don't have a car. But when you walk home. I know you're staying with the Briggses, but when you get your own place. Or even when you're just walking to the Briggses. The sunrise here is beautiful. It's slow rising. Over the hills on the other side of the valley across the river. The hills on the Andover side of Perth-Andover. The motel here is on the Perth side of Perth-Andover. The bridge takes you to the Andover side.

 The other good part about the job is that it's usually pretty quiet. That's the nice thing about starting your shift at midnight. Pretty quiet. You might get the odd call from a visitor, but that's it. Oh, and we're the bus stop, too, for the area, but the only bus that'll come by on your shift is the one coming back from Montreal, heading to Halifax. That usually gets here at about seven a.m., so you might get a few people needing to use the washrooms, which is fine. And the driver, he'll pick up any mail or packages we have for him. We keep all of the mail and packages together just under the desk here. As you can see, not very many. It's usually only one or two packages here for them. Usually not even that much. Any of the visitors call you in the night, well, the closet around the corner has extra towels and blankets. Ice buckets. If you want to take a smoke break, just walk out the front door here. We don't let the day staff do that, but the night shift can in between midnight and six a.m. I would bring a book. Or, I guess, you could bring a notepad and work on those stories you were telling me about. Not too bad of a job for that, huh? You could get all sorts of writing done here! You could write a book!

If you ever see anyone drive up and park in the lot, you don't have to approach them. If you see anyone parking and they're suspicious, you can just call the RCMP. The detachment is really close by, so they don't mind checking it out for you. Sometimes, you'll get drivers pulling in here to sleep in their cars overnight. Nothing major. RCMP will wake them up for you, get them moving again. Really though, I don't care if people pull in here and sleep in their vehicles. Better than them getting into an accident and hurting themselves or someone else. I had a friend, once, he'd fallen asleep driving. He said he remembered he was behind the wheel driving, and the next thing he knew he was waking up in the hospital seven months later. He'd been in a coma. Fell asleep at the wheel and the car went off the road and into a tree. He was lucky, just had a head injury, but was all right once that healed up and he regained consciousness.

Actually, now that I think of it, that's not all he remembered. He didn't remember this until a while after he got out of the hospital. But he said, and this was months after he had woken up, he said he started remembering things from when he was in the coma. Like dreams. Except they weren't quite like dreams. He said they were almost like lucid-type dreams. Like choose your own adventures. He was dreaming, but he could make decisions in the dreams.

In one of the dreams . . . it's funny. I'd forgotten about this until now. I haven't spoken to this friend in like eight years or something. I'd forgotten all about this.

In one of these coma dreams, my friend was just walking through the woods. He was just walking around in the woods, but he was lost. No idea where he was. And then suddenly he comes into this clearing in the middle of the woods, and there's an old man standing in the middle of the clearing. And my friend, he didn't know how he knew this, you know how in dreams sometimes you just know things for some reason? Anyway, my friend, he said, as soon as he walked into this clearing, as soon as he saw this old man, he knew the old man was God. Like, the Lord. God. And God handed him these three big books. And so my friend, he opened the books, and all of the pages in the books, they were completely blank. And so he asked God why he was giving him these three books. He told God he didn't understand.

And so God, this old man, told him. God said to my friend that each one of the books represented my friend's life. And God was going to give him three chances to write a life with a happy ending.

And then all of a sudden, my friend was an embryo again. Inside of his mother's womb. And he was born again. And he was an infant again, and then he was a toddler again, and so on. My friend had to live his life all over again, but while he was in the coma.

He told me that the dream time worked liked actual time. Like, as he had to go through life again each time . . . that it took as long as it did in real life. And all the decisions he made mattered. And that he got to make different decisions than he had in his real life.

So the first time he does this, he goes through his life again, he ends up getting married and then divorced. And right after he gets divorced, he dies from a heart attack when he's running this marathon. And after he dies, he finds himself back in the clearing in the woods. And God is standing there. And God takes one of the books out of his hands. And the book turns to ash. And God, the old man, says to him, "Two books left."

And then my friend is inside of his mother's womb again. And so he goes through his entire life again in real time, again while still in the coma. And this time, he's really depressed and feeling really scared about failing at his life again. And the pressure on him it gets so intense that he starts using cocaine and he gets addicted to cocaine. And he winds up in this fight with this drug dealer in Halifax. And the drug dealer stabs him. And all of a sudden he's back in the clearing. With God. The old man.

And God takes another book from him. And the book turns to ash. "One book left."

And my friend, he finds himself in his mother's womb again. But this time, something is different. All of a sudden, the dream, it's not a choose your own adventure anymore. The dream, all of a sudden, it's not a lucid dream anymore. He has to live his life all over again. In real time, like he did in real life. Before he was in the car accident. Before he was in the coma. So he's like a prisoner inside himself. Watching himself make all of those original choices again. Watching himself make all of those decisions again. And so it comes to the night where he's driving on the highway at night. And he falls asleep. And then, all of a sudden, he's in that clearing in the woods with God again.

And so God looks at him. And then he looks at the book my friend is holding. The last book. And then God looks at my friend again. And God looks into my friend's eyes.

My friend told me that that's when he woke up outta his coma. Crazy, eh?

And I only remembered that because you were telling me about those stories you were working on, almost like you were trying to write some book of your own, eh?

Aren't you?

Right now, the sun is rising around eight o'clock on the dot. Pretty much exactly when you get off work, so you got some nice end-of-shift walks ahead of ya.

Best part of the shift, you ask me.

See the beginning of each and every brand new day that ever was.

You are going to need to get that haircut, though. There's a barber in town. Over on the Andover side.

4.

EVA, 33 (PERTH–ANDOVER, NB)

All right. Now? Now talk? Yes? Talk now, yes?

Eva. Bouma. I'm thirty-three years old and originally from Shediac. But I am working now as a massage therapist here in Perth-Andover, because my husband got a job up here through Canadian Forest Services. And the reason I am here to talk to you is because my friend Keith Forrest told me I should come here and talk to you and tell you my story because you're trying to write a book.

Keith can be a bit of a weirdo sometimes, but he's also a really nice guy. If he gave you a job, you know that already. He was pretty insistent on me talking to you, so here it goes . . .

There is something happening here in Perth-Andover. Something major. And no one really knows what it is. Just to preface, so you know a little bit about Perth-Andover, this has always been a pretty quiet place. It's a small community. Like a lot of the other communities up and down the river valley. Except we're bigger than a place like Bath, or even Florenceville, really.

Where I work, we're right along the river on the Andover side here of Perth-Andover. And lately, I mean for the past two weeks, really, the number of times the RCMP or the paramedics or the fire trucks have sped past the parlour with their sirens going has started to get crazy. They're going by a lot. They're going by so often it makes me feel like something is going on.

So one of my clients, he's a reporter. And I was giving him a massage on Saturday, and the RCMP went screaming by the parlour, and he remarked about it, so we got to talking about it while I was giving him his massage.

So my client, he tells me that people are going missing up upriver and that the people up there are freaking out. And my client, he tells me, it's not like a couple of people have gone missing. My client says that over fifteen people have gone missing from the reserve in the last month.

And according to him, he says the RCMP have no idea what's going on up there, either. He said, they figured it must have been some kind of a gang thing, or one family up there fighting another one, because you know how politics can kind of get a bit crazy on the reserve sometimes. But he said he went up there himself and he says it's not like that at all. He says people up there are genuinely scared about what's happening. He says it's not drug related. He says it's not some kind of family feud. He says the men up there are loading their shotguns and putting them beside their beds at night. He says the Elders up there are telling everyone to not leave their houses after dark, and not to let their children out of their sight.

And the RCMP, they've taken the dogs up there. They've been sending the planes overhead with the infrared. But they don't know what's happening. And they aren't talking to the press or anyone else about it. Neither are the paramedics or the fire department. No one'll talk about it. Except for a few of the Elders upriver because they're scared for their community.

Now, my client works for the newspaper. And of course, all the newspapers in New Brunswick are owned by the Irvings. So you don't know for one hundred percent it isn't the Irvings just trying to drum up some kind of panic through the media. I read that in a Naomi Klein book once. How corporations like drumming up emergency situations in certain places because it's easier to operate and get things in place if people are all riled up and scared and the like. I don't know if the Irvings have ever wanted to buy land up near the reserve or what. Or if that has anything to do with what's going on right now.

But something is happening. Something is sending those vehicles upriver with the sirens going. It's never been this often before. Even that last big flood we had, the sirens weren't going this often.

And that flood nearly ended us. It nearly took everything we ever had from us.

So something must be going on.

And my client he says there is going to be this big exposé about it in the paper this week. Again, hopefully, this isn't just some kind of scheme the Irvings are pulling.

This community, we got real untrustful about a lot of things after that last flood. Floods are horrible things. They destroy communities.

Maybe there's some kind of explanation for it, something really silly like a bunch of people getting together and deciding to go have a party somewhere and it got out of hand or something, I don't know.

But when the rational explanations you try coming up with start sounding more fantastic than the irrational ones, that's when you . . . I don't know . . . figure out what's going on and let people know about it so that . . . everyone's not living in the dark, you know? People who live in the dark all the time, they end up going crazy, don't they?

I mean, unless that's your job, I mean. Working all night. The graveyard shift.

But that's not was I was talking about. It's not what I'm here to talk about.

People have trouble murdering one person and getting rid of the evidence. How you could murder fifteen and hide the evidence . . . I don't think it's even possible.

Is it?

5.

SABRINA, 28 (PERTH-ANDOVER, NB)

White people pretending things aren't how they really are has been going on for as long as we've known them. This is not something new. This is something as old as our relationship. It's like speaking make-believe talking to white people. And their accents are so thick you can see it happening in them. When they start talking about equality or saying "we're all the same," you can see it in their eyes. Right in the dark part of their eyes. Part of them, some little part of them never really believes that. They always know they're different. Just like you, right now; I can see it there. Sitting down in the dark part, the beady black of your pupil. It's there. That knowledge. And I don't know anymore if it's even something they can help or not. Because I can see it in every white person when I talk to them. Every single one. This knowledge they got in the pupil of their eye. The dark part of their soul. The part, let's face it, that was relieved when we all started dying from diseases when they got here. The part that some of them don't acknowledge even exists but that we all know it does because we got eyes, too. Eyes like theirs, except we can see.

So a bunch of white people not making a big deal of out a bunch of missing Indigenous people, that part of the whole thing don't surprise me. It's not like it hasn't happened before. Indigenous people going missing or getting murdered or raped and white people not giving a fuck. But what I don't get is why they aren't making a big deal out of this because this shit is happening just upriver. The reserve is so close to here. It's literally just upriver a bit. Very close to where white people live. So why the hell aren't people making a big deal of it down here? Why isn't it in the paper? I was speaking to a reporter just last week! What happened to him? He said he was writing a story about it. Unless somebody found out he was writing a story about it and didn't want him to. I mean, everybody knows the Irvings; they own all the newspapers in New Brunswick. Maybe they don't want people getting riled up around here for some kind of business reason, who knows. And maybe they're telling the government to keep things hush-hush about it, because everyone knows Irving controls the government, too, and . . . why isn't anyone talking about it?

We hooked up in university, me and James, my husband. Over in school in Presque Isle. Just finished our degrees and James decides he wants to come back here. Come back home. To the reserve. Put his education to good use. He decided he wanted to make a difference.

So we move back to the reserve. We start living the life again. And James, he wants to shake everything up, get involved in the politics, make some changes to the place. Well, that went over like a brick through a church window. They weren't so receptive to it. If you can understand . . . see, we moved away from the reserve. We moved away with no plans of returning. People thought of us as gone for good. And then one day we show up again, out of the blue, with James on a mission, on some kind of crusade to fix the place . . .

People don't like outsiders telling them how to fix their own shit. And here I am, stuck with such a man.

I never wanted to come back. I came back for James.

And we got the shit treatment pretty soon after that. And James wouldn't listen to me, he wouldn't tone down his act at all and so . . . and so. Sometimes people will spray paint your house. Sometimes people will pour sugar in the gas tank of your truck. Sometimes people will pretend like you don't exist.

They're all huddled together now. The ones that are left up there. They're hunkering down, patrolling the streets in their warrior garb. Driving their ATVs around. They barricaded the entrances, started a couple of bonfires . . . you can see them from across the river, if you drive up the Andover side a ways. With the barricades, no one gets in or out, except for residents or the RCMP because they have to let them through.

But their patrols and their barricades aren't worth shit. They found our truck on the side of the road inside the perimeter of those barricades. James had gone out to gas up the truck, because the gas station is right outside of the perimeter. So he passed back through the barricades to drive back home. He must have. But he never made it. Whatever it is got to him before he could come home to me.

And because it was James, right? I mean, the Elders, everyone they made the proper noises, they all said, well, he's our brother, and we will never give up on him, we will find him, we will never stop looking and all of that, but I mean, really? I know. I know how they feel. I believe some people were happy he was gone.

And that's why I left. That's why I'm here. I was born on that reserve, sure. But I sure as hell am not going to die there. Not with them. Let them defend the place themselves.

Just his truck on the side of the road. Key still in the ignition. Lights still on. Engine still running.

It doesn't happen. It can't happen, today. It's impossible. And nobody has any answers.

And the RCMP and the government don't know anything? No, thank you. No, thank you.

I hope you take what I'm saying right now, that you take it and tell everyone you know. Tell every single other white person out there that something is happening to us, and because they're handling it the way they are . . . this will hurt them. This kind of thing breaks trust between the races. Between people.

As if there was any left.

I think we're all in a lot of trouble. I think we're all screwed. You tell them that.

6.

LORNE, 26 (PERTH–ANDOVER, NB)

I couldn't get comfortable on the bus. I'm too big for the seats, that headrest is just a little too low, the round part of it presses against that bump on the lower part of my skull in the back, so every little bump the bus hits kind of bounces my head off the headrest, and it pretty much sucked. Once you get to Ontario, the buses change. They're run by a different company or something. I like the Ontario buses better. I can get comfortable in those seats better.

I'm coming straight from Toronto, so yeah, a little sleep would have been okay. Kind of a long trip without sleep. But there's something calming about riding in the bus in the middle of the night. When they turn off the lights, and you can turn on the overhead fan, and there's just those little hallway mini lights that are on. It's easier on the eyes. And the cool air from the fan is nice. I can just kind of pop on my headphones and kind of coast through the night. Look out at the landscape through the windows. Last night was pretty clear so I could kind of look at the moon and the stars and everything. If it wasn't for the bus seat it would have been great. I tried putting my jacket underneath my head as a pillow, but I couldn't ever seem to get it just right for some reason. But other than my seat, it was nice.

I had lots to think about anyway with my grandfather dying and all that. He passed away in the home over in Andover. That was just a couple of days ago. It was apparently pretty peaceful, natural. So. When Dad called me, I wasn't expecting it. For a bunch of reasons. First, because me and Dad don't get along, and he never calls me and we don't talk much. Even when he called me, that was a ten-second conversation. "Your grandfather's dead." "Okay, I'll take the bus and be there Friday morning." Click.

Gramps had been in the home so long I just kind of got used to . . . this sounds bad, but I just kind of got used to him being old and away from us, like in the home . . . and I didn't really get around to visiting him that much, so part of me kind of took it for granted and part of me must have kind of just gotten used to him always being there. I know that sounds bad, but I've been thinking about it on the bus . . . I took it for granted, his being in the home. You know how when you live in the city, you kind of stop looking at the stars? Because of the light pollution in the city, you can't see as many, so the light pollution makes them appear fainter and farther away, and so after a while you just kind of stop looking at the stars? The cityscape kind of becomes your stars after a while. You stop looking at the stars and start looking at the cityscape and the cityscape becomes your stars. But the stars are still up there. They're burning as bright as they ever have. Past the smog and the light pollution. But you kind of stop thinking about them.

On the bus ride back here, that stretch between Rivière-du-Loup and Edmundston, that's dark country. You get to see the stars again. Start to remember what they were. Start to remember how beautiful they were. How much they meant to you. How much you loved them.

So the city . . . I like the city. I like Toronto. I got right wrapped up in Toronto.

I know it sounds bad, but I forgot about Gramps.

Kind of like my parents seem to have forgotten about me now. Which is totally weird, because usually if Dad doesn't want to pick me up, Mom is here with the van.

I'm sure I told Dad Friday.

The bus only comes east this time in the morning.

I can wait a few more minutes. You don't mind if I grab a coffee?

I got buddies in town from growing up. Someone will come get me. At some point.

The only thing I really ever miss about Toronto, though, is the amount of people there. The stars aren't as bright, but you're always surrounded by people. I find that's the hardest thing to adjust to when you leave the city. How there's so few people around you.

Especially here in New Brunswick. The population problem, everyone leaving for out west.

Because this place is dead. Relatively, at least.

Dad and me don't get along, but they're always here, usually.

Maybe the van broke down.

NOVEMBER

LOWELL (TRANS-CANADA HIGHWAY, NB)

The wolf stories . . . I'm stuck right now. I don't know where to take them next.

People keep asking me if I'm a writer or a journalist. When I try to record them. I don't think I am, though. Either of those things. If I was, I wouldn't keep getting stuck on the wolf stories.

When I record people . . . it's about sound. Because I'm looking for sound.

The stories are just . . . distractions.

Everyone's asleep on the bus right now. Some old lady is snoring in the seat ahead of me. That's the sound around me. Someone's occasional coughing. The sound of bus tires rolling on the highway.

We'll be in Montreal first thing in the morning. Jane's in Montreal. Feelings and people.

But whatever that was happening in Perth-Andover . . . that riot or whatever upriver . . . I mean, if I had been from there or knew the area, it would have been less creepy. But because I was a stranger there, like, not familiar with the area and all the stories going around . . . that was what really made me anxious to get out of the place. It was pretty there and everything, and the people were really nice but . . .

Tonight, we left behind all of it. The bus drove right past it. The reserve, it's on the other side of the river from the highway we're on. Over on the Perth side, I guess. There were a whole bunch of bonfires over there, flickering. A bunch of bonfires and, well . . . flashing lights. Like police cars, those kind of . . . flashing lights. We just drove past it.

It's Halloween night, and I'm heading into Quebec.

Keith paid me more than he had to. More than I actually worked. I got decent money in my pockets again, finally.

It's going to be pretty cool to see Jane again.

I should probably get some sleep right now but I don't feel sleepy. I got used to working the graveyard shift.

The occasional cough. The sound of tires rolling on the highway.

Goodnight, tape recorder. Get some rest, tape recorder.

Feelings and people. Goodnight.

1.

WANDA, 24 (RIVIÈRE-DU-LOUP, QC)

I'm travelling to Ottawa to go to visit my sister. She keeps sending me and my family all of these emails about weird stuff happening in Ottawa, so my parents asked me to go and visit her and make sure she's still taking her medication and to bring her back to New Brunswick if she's gone crazy this time for real. She's a real free spirit.

But I'm talking to Lowell now because he asked me if he could record me, and I said yes, because I have a story that I'd like to pitch him and get his feedback on because he tells me he's been writing stories, too.

Once upon a time, there was a beautiful girl named Melinda. And she was a mermaid. And she lived in the ocean, and rode on dolphins, and fell in love with the prince of Atlantic, Prince Finley. Unfortunately for Melinda, however, Prince Finley was royalty, the prince of the kingdom, and she was just a regular mermaid with no royal blood and didn't have any seashells to her name hardly at all. Seashells are the currency they use in Atlantis.

And there was this royal ball that was held every year in Atlantis that the King of Atlantis put on that all of the rich mermaids got invited to so that they could dance with the king's son, the prince. And if the prince decided he wanted to marry any of the girls at the dance he could. But year after year, they held this dance, and year after year, the prince never found a mermaid he liked. And Melinda never got to go to these mermaid dances because she never had enough seashells to buy an outfit. But then, one day, her friend, Sammy the Seahorse came up with an idea to rob the First Atlantis

National Bank. And he asked Melinda to help him rob the place. And Melinda was poor because she didn't have many seashells and was barely scraping by and had to eat seaweed her whole life and didn't have any pearls to wear. So Melinda decides to help Sammy the Seahorse rob the bank. And they get Carl the Crab to help them. Because Carl owns a trident store and they need tridents to hold up the other mermaids in the bank. And so they walk into the bank one day, with their tridents—

This is how the story starts. I'm trying to develop it into a screenplay. I have a friend at school who's going to help me. His name is Brett Bell. He's a writer. Like, an actual writer. And I've always loved mermaids. And he wants to get into film. And I have a lot of ideas. And film is really big now. And if we don't try and make it into a full-length film, we might try and make it into a TV show because I'm pretty sure the story is pretty original. I haven't seen anything like it. See, because Melinda wants to go to this dance so bad she becomes a bank robber with her friends. But then things get complicated because there's this humpback whale that's like, the best detective in Atlantis, and he's really old, but really smart, like Columbo. Wally the Humpback Whale. And he starts tracking them down after they rob the bank because Carl the Crab dropped his wallet in the bank when they were robbing it. But Melinda's really likeable, too, so Wally starts to feel really conflicted about trying to arrest her. Because she never uses all the seashells for herself. She only uses enough seashells to buy a dress and some nice shoes and some pearls and a dolphin carriage so she can get into the royal dance so she can dance with the prince. The rest of the seashells she gives to charity. So she's kind of like Robin Hood in a way. And Wally the Humpback Whale kind of respects her for that, you know, because his parents were poor when he grew up, and being poor is really tough on whales because they have to eat so much to maintain their body weight and stay healthy.

I already know the story is original. I know nobody's written anything like it before because it's like a mermaid version of *Breaking Bad* because the more and more banks she robs the more trouble she gets into. And then Sammy the Seahorse gets shot, during this big heist. And she gets really sad. And they have to go to his funeral and pay their respects without getting caught by the police—

In Montreal, they have a mermaid school. Did you know that? It's a school, where you put on a tail, and they teach you how to swim like a mermaid.

So all the resources are there. To do a show. Like, you can teach actors how to swim like mermaids and you wouldn't even have to green screen it. Or use any CGI.

And the story's really universal because most countries in the world are next to the ocean. So everyone knows about Atlantis and all of that.

The hardest part will be getting a big name actor for the King of Atlantis, but whoever plays him, has to be epic. Like Gary Oldman or something. But once we get someone like that on board, the CBC would be idiots not to pick up the show or make it into a movie.

And I know I'm talking a lot about it, but I've been putting a lot of time into it is why. And Brett Bell, he's been helping me write it, and we already have the character biographies written up for everyone and the synopsis and everything.

And I think there's some people in Ottawa who know film, too, and theatre, so when I get there . . . I mean, part of the trip is going to my friend's wedding, but part of it is also going to be networking, trying to meet any industry people I can, and trying to sell them on it.

And I mean, I'm from Rothesay, right? New Brunswick. So it's a pretty big deal, if I can get it going. And if we can shoot the show in New Brunswick, it'll mean all of these jobs for the economy, and because the economy in New Brunswick's so bad now, it would really help create jobs and build the economy so it's going to be really awesome once we start filming.

What do you think? As a writer.

Be honest.

My sister is fine. It's Ottawa, for God's sake. What kind of bad could be happening in Ottawa?

2.

HUBERT, 54 (TROIS-RIVIÈRES, QC)

I seen you, several times there in Perth. Working the desk. That motel. You remember? I'm sure I saw you there a couple of weeks ago. What's happening down there, now? Something going on down there. Not sure what but something.

Up this way, it's more quiet. Not much going on. Just the valley and trees and the dark. Sometimes, now, at night, there are lights in the dark. Have you seen them? I have seen them twice now. Do you know what I am talking about?

When we stop here at this place, I get the déjeuner. Breakfast. Early bird. Even though we get here around three a.m. Early bird, for sure. Early bird, that's me. That's all of us. Getting the good breakfast before all of the people who live here in this community wake up. The three a.m. early bird special.

Do you know how a girl, in her jeans, they make the ass look smaller? It's true. When a girl, she wears her jeans, and she know it makes her ass look smaller.

Most times, I am here alone. Bus driver. Not everyone want to talk to me. My English not so good mais je suis bilingue. Eh? You understand me? Most people from Nouveau Brunswick sont anglophones, ne voulait parler avec moi-çi. I am just the bus driver. *Driving Miss Daisy*. Because anglophones, they think the world belongs to them. But not in this place-çi. Not in this dark province.

Do you know how a fish, in a cave, the cave there is no light, and the fish, their skin begins to glow in the dark? In time. Through the evolution. And their eyes turn white. They begin to see in the dark? Do you know how a deer, on the road, crosses and the lights of the bus they catch, and the deer doesn't move? Looks into the lights as the bus drives right through its body?

Do you know I have a grandkid? And my grandkid, she ask me what it is like to drive a bus? And I tell her it's good. I make good money. I get to travel.

I am lying to her, though, my grandkid. I don't make good money. I don't get to travel.

You might think, what do you mean? You are a bus driver. You are always on the road. And yes. That's true. But I am always in the bus. I am in the bus, and I get off at the stops to pick up the parcels and mail and to eat the early bird meals, sure. But they are these little dots on the map, whenever I get off. The scenery it is like a movie. Always behind the screen. I do not travel. I am always on the bus. In some ways, I travel less than people who never leave their neighbourhood. It is just a job. It is just work. And the money is not good.

Do you know how a deer on the road looks into the lights as the bus passes through?

Do you know how a fish in a cave begins to see in the dark?

3.

OMAR, 28 (MONTREAL, QC)

There are rumblings, rumblings all over the place up here. It's not a good thing.

You can tell by talking to the street kids that's how you can tell. Normally, that's the last thing you want, to talk to them. All sorts of crazy and have to watch your wallet, but me, I got my chain, it's all attached, and I know if anyone tries to grab it, I can just use my Greco-Roman-style wrestling and that's it for them, so I don't feel fear talking to the punks.

You get used to them, like landmarks. Because they have their favourite spots and usually go the same places at the same times in the day and at night, and it becomes ritualistic for them, like their culture so you can see them do that. And the cops . . . the cops can try and clear them out, but it's really like trying to shoo away pigeons.

With pigeons, think about pigeons. Think about pigeons, sir. This isn't a forest. This is a city. This place is steel and concrete and flashing lights and people who don't give a fuck. And pigeons, sir. Everywhere. All over. Living. Surviving. In large herds, sir. For years, sir. They live here. Because they live around us, sir. That is their magic trick. They don't live with us. They live around us. That is evolution, sir. True, working evolution. Finding a way around things, sir. Finding a way. They do not conquer. They do not fight. They live around us.

Like the street kids. The ones who survive. They find a way. They live around, not with. They squeegee the cars whether you ask them to or not and, if you tell them to fuck off, they barely even hear you, sir. Your voice barely even registers. They move on to the next car. Until the lights turn. And they survive.

The cops come and they sit there and if the cops go hard, they scatter. And the cops leave and they come back. Just like the pigeons, sir. Just like the birds.

And just like the birds, you can tell if something is wrong with your city, by looking at the street kids. If they stop congregating. If they dwindle in numbers.

And they are dwindling. There are less of them about. On the streets. And they are talking about it, in the shelters. And the cops are talking about it, too. You hear them talking about it on the street. You can see the look in their eyes. You can hear pieces of it on their radios.

They are speaking softer to the street kids, now. They do not shoo them away anymore. And they watch them now. Concern in their eyes. They ask them questions because they are curious. Because they see it. Just like I see it. There is something wrong with the street kids, sir. Because they are going missing. Even though the pigeons are not.

Something is happening. You look up at the cross on the mountain at night and wonder how it can shine so brightly. How can the cross be shining? How is it shining when something like this is happening? Speak with the street kids. They will tell you. They don't know what it is, but they will tell you.

I will not go walking at night anymore in certain places. And I am a big man. And I know Greco-Roman-style wrestling. But I will not go walking at night no more.

But I am lucky. Because the street kids, they have to walk. At night, they have to walk and it is not good. Some of them refuse to go to the shelter, and that is not good. And they are going missing.

Where are they going?

There is nowhere they can go.

There is nowhere for them to go, so they are going into the air.

It's not good, where they are going.

I don't see how it can be good.

4.

LOU, 59 (MONTREAL, QC)

Some children, they do not remember, they have never had that experience. And this makes me sad. I never had that experience when I was a child, but I had it later in life, when it came to me. I did not follow les sport when I was a child. I was very much a nerd or a geek, and I read beaucoup, beaucoup de livres. That was my thing. I liked the language. I liked the texts in books.

And my father he never showed an interest either, same as me. He was a teacher, he taught the maths à l'école. Plus de quarante ans. For more than forty years, he was a teacher of maths. But when he got le cancer du poumon, because he smoked les cigarettes, and he was admitted to l'hôpital, after this, he became interested in the game. He became interested in baseball. This was in '82. When he was sick. We put un radio dans son chambre à l'hôpital, et il toujours listened to les jeux des Expos. This was not something he had ever done before. His whole life, which I had ever witnessed. Et I was twenty-four years of age in '82. And every once in a while, we got to take him, my father, to the stadium Olympique to watch les Expos.

And when we would get there in the stadium and in our seats, we would watch the game. And my father he would watch with both eyes wide like a child's. Like he was seeing something for the first time. This baseball. And you know how they say that the closer you get to death, the more you become like a child? I believe this is what was happening to my father. I believe he was becoming like a child. Because a child looks at the world like it is magic. Like they are full with wonder. This is what my father was like. And this was in '82. We began to take my father to games. And les Expos were doing better in '82. Like they were waking up after a bunch of disappointing saisons. But even though they were doing better, they did not win every game. People were used to this, in Montréal. People would hope for the best, but expected to lose. And if les Expos lost the game, it was not la fin du monde. Because there was always tomorrow. There would always be another game tomorrow. And this is how people thought. But my father, whenever we took him to a game, and les Expos they would start to be losing, he would start talking to himself out loud. Talking to himself but you could hear him. "Où est le Grand Orange?" he would say to no one. "Où est le Grand Orange?" I did not know what he was trying to say. I did not know, and when I asked him, he would just look at me like I was the crazy one. So I had to end up asking my friend who was a fan of baseball this question, "Qui est le Grand Orange?" And my friend he smiled at me and said, "Rusty Staub." Rusty Staub had been a player for les Expos years earlier, a man with red hair and the first superstar of les Expos. He was a hero from the past. And my father must have remembered him, and that is why he was saying that whenever les Expos began to lose.

If you look at it, the stadium, it looks very odd. It looks like the corpse of some animal that has began to rot after it dies. The tower looks like when the flesh gets eaten away clean and a white bone sticks up through the corpse. The designer of the stadium, he designed it to look like the vertebrae of un animal, and that is how I think of it now. They built it dans le parc et vraiment, it looks like the bones of un animal you would come across if you were hunting. The corpse of un animal in a field.

I would think of this whenever we would go to watch the games there with les Expos. How you know how sometimes, a young child will find the dead body of un animal for the first time in their lives and play with it. Because they don't know what it is. It is just an object to them. Or how a child will play in a graveyard and step on the graves because they do not know. We would go to the games to watch les Expos, and my father looking like a child, and feeling like we were all gathered together in this big skeleton, you know? Playing games like children inside the skeleton of some dead animal gigantesque. I think this is how the designer wanted it. Because how in life the flowers and plants will grow up around a dead body, and life will flourish there, and insects will live in the corpse, and the plants will grow up through the body, you know? I think that is what the designer was thinking.

My father died quickly. He did not make it à la saison prochaine. But I kept going to the games from then on. For him. It was for him. Because I think that, at the end of his life, he had regrets, you know, that he had grown up too fast et il . . . missed out on something . . . you know, in his childhood.

And there are many people who complain about les Expos. Et le stadium. Because it cost the people here so much money, you know. One and a half billion dollars. It is a lot. A lot to pay for a pile of bones. Des os blancs d'un animal gigantesque.

When they left, les Expos, they left the stadium behind. Too big to take with them, you know?

I still go out to les os blancs, now. Once every couple of weeks to see the place with my eyes again, you know? I take le metro to Pie-IX on the Green Line, to see with my own eyes the graveyard that used to house les Expos, all of the life at that time.

And it feels like the place is waiting, you know? It doesn't feel like it is finished. It feels like it is waiting. Like a promise.

"Où est le Grand Orange?"

5.

NIKKI, 27 (MONTREAL, QC)

We think it's gotta be like some kind of cult. Like, some kind of Freemason-type thing that's been organizing itself secretly for years. That's the only explanation we can come up with. Because whoever it is that's behind it, they've got their fingers into everything. Especially the media. Not just the news, but social media and . . . I mean, you see some people posting about the strangeness going on a little here and there and the odd guy ranting about it, but those posts, have you noticed? They're not staying up for very long. That's why there's no panic yet or you know, that kind of thing. Someone's working things from behind the scenes, that has their fingers everywhere, and they're trying to keep whatever's going on, or whatever they themselves are up to with the bodies and the kidnappings . . . they're trying to keep it all hush-hush. They might even be listening to us now. And I know that's a real cliché line to say, but I think it might actually be true, in this case. Some groups of people are powerful enough that they actually might be listening to us right now in this hostel. Through the use of satellites or whatever the technology exists, we know that, already, so if these people, cult, whatever they are, Freemasons, are in positions of power, then why couldn't they be using this technology to keep whatever plot or operation right now under wraps and listening for people who might be talking about it to get rid of them pre-emptively, you know?

You should walk real careful and keep your nose down. If they, whoever they are, know you're walking around with a tape recorder, who knows, they might target you, think you're up to something that might ruin, get in the way of whatever the fuck their plans are.

What do you think their plans are?

My boyfriend said he would text me a half an hour ago. He still hasn't texted me. He's in Manitoba. Why hasn't he texted me? What's going on in Manitoba right now? It's been a half an hour. And I don't think I'm overreacting here. I came here from Labrador, and you gotta drive through the wilderness to get to here from Labrador, and let me tell you . . . something ain't right. The people in Labrador were fuckin' spooked. They were not their friendly Newfie selves this time around when I went there to make the drop. Heroin. To my buddy's friend. For my buddy. Not my boyfriend, he's a surveyor, he doesn't know my on-the-side stuff I do for my buddy. Because you can't abandon your friends, you know, when they need you, and my car still works, right? Doesn't matter if you're in a relationship or not. And my buddy paid me in coke so, especially considering how much coke it was, I couldn't turn it down. You try being in a relationship with a guy who takes off for six weeks at a time to go surveying in Manitoba. What the hell is there to survey in Manitoba, even? That's another good question.

Here's another tip. Never do coke in your own apartment. Learned that a long time ago. If you get any coke, go to a hostel. If your boyfriend's in Manitoba, he'll never find out. Because you never meet anyone you know in a hostel, you know?

We could be next, that's what I'm getting at. That's my ultimate point. And if we post something about it on Facebook, someone's going to unpost it, you get me? Like, maybe the Freemasons.

Try it. Try posting it on Facebook. I'm not. Fuck that, I discontinued my account.

And I don't talk to anyone I don't know anymore. I never talk to people in hostels.

Except you. Because you gotta talk to somebody or else you become a crazy person.

What was your name again?

6.

DWIGHT, 37 (MONTREAL, QC)

I had asked her if she could cook us up some meatballs, sweet and sour meatballs, because I've always liked meatballs, and she was a real good cook. And her meatballs were awesome. And we hadn't had them in a while, because money has been tight for the last little while, but I got this pay raise recently, and so it was just after I had got the pay raise, like a couple of days after that, and we were ahead of our bills, and I wasn't feeling too stressed out about anything, and I think she could sense that. And she was kind of more relaxed than usual as well, probably because I was more relaxed, so she was able to relax more. So we were a little more relaxed than we have been this year, and we were actually enjoying each other's company and having fun around each other again. So I asked her if she'd cook some meatballs that night.

We'd first met about six years ago. Both of us old enough that we were sick of the bar scene, and really didn't want to expose ourselves to the dating pool anymore. I think maybe that helped us get going and stick together through all of that early-phase turbulence a lot of couples can't seem to make it through. But, after a while, we really started to kind of unexpectedly love each other. Like, I'm not sure what our designs were, when we first started up. What designs we had originally placed upon each other.

But we fell in love at some point there, after we kind of found ourselves a way into it and so . . . yeah, we were very happy—a bit stressed because of bills, but happy. There's kind of a happy stressed-out kind of way you can carry on like, once you get the hang of it. This happy sort of stressed out kind of everything sucks, but what are you going to do type of way of living.

And when a little breather happens, when a little bit of the stress goes away, due to one person getting a raise or one person having something good finally happen to them that day . . . it's really welcome, first off, these little breaks from the stress . . . but it also . . . gives you a chance to . . . remember all the love and stuff you're feeling for each other. And that's what was happening to me and Alison. Because the raise I got gave us just enough to clear a little bit more of our bills a bit. Like we had been holding our breath for ages and finally had a chance to just breathe a little bit again.

And her cooking was amazing, so I wanted her meatballs. And she actually wanted to make them for me that night, so she did. And I don't know what she put in them. Like onions and peppers, obviously. Like the ingredients I could see, obviously I knew what those were. But there was more going into her meatballs than just onions and peppers. Because you could tell when she cooked them, first off. And second, when you put them in your mouth and began to chew and all of the flavour . . . she had some kind of secret ingredient that she used in them. And whenever I asked her what the secret ingredient was, she'd always just say "love." And that was funny, to her and to me because we'd always been real sarcastic people. And that was just about the lamest thing either of us had ever heard, whenever one of those morons on the Food Network would say that they were cooking with love. Literally, the dumbest thing we'd ever heard.

She'd say "love." And I would tell her to shut up. And she'd laugh about it. And it would make me smile, when she laughed. Because I knew how stupid we both thought that was of a thing to say, when you're asking about food. Because food is just work, right? It's all preparation and focus and timing and attention to detail and heat. Having the proper ingredients and tools to get the job done in the first place. In reality.

The meatballs that night were pretty good. They weren't her best. The glaze wasn't as sweet as she normally made it, whatever. They were still pretty good.

We went to bed that night, and I couldn't sleep. So I read from my science fiction book, because I like science fiction, while Alison eventually got in bed and fell right asleep beside me. *Children of Dune.* By Frank Herbert. And I finished the book, that night, came to the last page, read the sentence, that last sentence that you know goes . . . but it wasn't my first time reading the book before. I'd read it already, like, six times before then. This was my seventh time finishing it.

I let the book fall off the bed, 'cause it was a softcover, I reached down to scratch my knee because it was itchy, then I brought my hand up again to turn the knob of the lamp on the nightstand beside the bed. Turned off the light. Listened to Alison breathing beside me in the dark. Listened to Alison breathing beside me in the dark, she's beside me, breathing, we're in the dark together and she's breathing . . . breathing in and out and breathing, I can hear her breathing, hear it now in my mind just hear her breathing—

I woke up in the morning, and she wasn't breathing anymore. And her body was cold.

And because of all the stories I'd been hearing, about people . . . going missing and such, I couldn't leave the room to go get my phone because I'd left it downstairs beside hers on the kitchen table the night before when I'd gone to bed. Because I was an idiot. I didn't want to leave her side, and have her go missing. How corny is that, right? Me, this intelligent guy, and knowing that all these stories we're hearing about people disappearing . . . knowing it's all bullshit, tacky, superstitious but still . . . being afraid because I didn't want . . . I was afraid if I left the room her body . . . her . . . corpse . . . to get my phone to call the hospital that she might not be . . . her body might not be . . . there. If I left and came back. Because I love her. I do love her.

So I couldn't not go and get my phone. Not for some stupid reason like that. Because of superstitions. Or fear. Or foolishness. I had to call someone. The hospital. You know?

I went downstairs to get my phone from the table. And then I went back upstairs.

We were laughing, the night before, about putting "love" into the meatballs. Because that's not what really happens. That's not a real thing.

Her body was gone. I came back, her body was gone.

DECEMBER

LOWELL (MONTREAL, QC)

Montreal is huge and awesome.

The Metro trains. How they rumble. The cathedral bells. Different languages drifting through the air. The place is so alive. So many people. Feelings and people.

I'm heading over to Jane's place tonight. This will be my second time seeing her since I've been here. We got together for a quick coffee a few days ago, but she was busy trying to wrap up her sessional course things whatever they're called and was working for some of the professors marking papers and stuff. Now that classes at McGill are done, now we get to hang out. So yeah. Yeah, I'm happy.

I need to figure out some kind of a gift for her or something. I don't know. What do girls even like? I don't want it to be weird. Maybe I shouldn't get a gift. Maybe I should just show up.

Food. I'll bring her food.

Because that's what a wolf would do, if she was part of his pack.

1.

JANE, 26 (MONTREAL, QC)

JANE: This time of the night, the street outside used to be way busier. This whole part of town has never been quiet like this before. Look down. I understand that you're coming here from Nova Scotia, but that? That is quiet for Montreal.

Sorry, where was I? Okay, right . . . so . . . the Fermi paradox.

The Fermi paradox is a problem posed by Italian physicist Enrico Fermi that scientists have been struggling to explain ever since the 1950s.

The problem is framed as thus:

When a person walks outside at night and looks up at the sky, they will see thousands of stars. But every star a person can see in the night sky . . . those are just the nearby stars. We can see only a little bit of the universe from Earth. And it is estimated that there are probably somewhere between one hundred to four hundred billion stars in our galaxy.

That's one hundred to four hundred billion stars in our galaxy, alone. Each one potentially the centre of its own solar system. And for every one of those stars, there could exist another entire galaxy outside of our own. Pay attention, Lowell. It's going to be on the exam.

Here's an idea of the scale we're talking about. For every grain of sand on planet Earth, there exists more than ten thousand stars out there. And because the universe is so big, and there's so many stars out there, the odds of there being stars like our own sun, with planets like ours orbiting them, with all of the necessary conditions for life, temperatures, chemical deposits, and atmospheric requirements, is extremely high.

Even if a person was super conservative with their calculations of the odds against it, there should still be at least one hundred billion, trillion planets out there in the universe right now, that are really close to being Earth-like enough, with the correct ingredients required for life on them. Now, let's say that out of all of those planets, and let's be conservative again, let's estimate that out of all of those planets only one percent of them actually develop life. And out of that one percent, let's be even more conservative and say that only one percent of that one percent develops life that is actually allowed to advance to a level of sentience comparable to ours.

What the Fermi paradox is saying, is that even if the odds are completely stacked against life in the universe, there should still remain at least one hundred habitable planets with intelligent life like ours for every single grain of sand on planet Earth.

And so, if there is that much potential for life in our universe, where is everybody? Even if we are being conservative . . . adding up all of the factors out there, given the information we have . . . where is everyone?

You might be thinking maybe there is intelligent life out there, they just aren't technologically advanced enough to reach us yet. But think about this: the Earth, our sun, they're young when compared to many of the other stars and habitable planets out there. Some of them are billions of years older. If any of them had intelligent life out there and have survived billions of years, then it stands to reason that there should be a few of them, potentially thousands at the very least, in our galaxy alone that would have had the time to colonize the Milky Way before now.

So why haven't we picked up signals from any of them?

Conspiracy theorists say the government has been hiding the evidence of other life from us for years. But given the math, there should be so much evidence of life elsewhere that I don't think even the government could hide it all if they wanted to.

And so we have this paradox. If the math suggests that there should be all of this intelligent life out there, where is it all?

Which brings us to the Great Filter.

The idea of a Great Filter suggests that there is this wall that all intelligent life hits, at some point or another, and that nothing can get by it. Except by some kind of a fluke or miracle or something. Which may be why we haven't seen other life forms yet out there. Everything out there keeps running into this wall. It is the idea that a species will develop so far and then hit this wall that just stops all life in its tracks.

And if this Great Filter thing exists, and if it's real, it means one of three things. It means us, humans, all of humanity, we're either rare, first, or we're all doomed.

If we're rare, it means the filter is behind us. There's hardly anyone out there in the cosmos because hardly anyone makes it as far as we have. Because some time long ago on Earth, the Great Filter happened, and we managed to survive it, and there might be hope that we can just keep developing and growing as a species until we colonize the whole universe and so on.

If we're first, it means that we haven't run into other life forms simply because we're the first species to make it this far. Maybe there isn't even a Great Filter at all for us. We're just that lucky. We're just first.

And then there's the other possibility: we could be doomed. The Great Filter might not have happened yet. Maybe it's still ahead of us, and we are doomed. We haven't run into extraterrestrial life yet because there isn't any, because all life before us in the galaxy has hit this, and it's only a matter of time before we do, too.

Okay, I need a refill. Drink break! Just one sec. Ah. Yeah. Okay. Where was I?

There could be all sorts of other possibilities, too, why we haven't encountered life. But the Great Filter idea is the one that always creeps me out. How there might be some kind of force, or event, or thing out there that is just . . . silencing life.

Which is why all this stuff going on right now here in Montreal . . . and those reports on the news yesterday about that all-of-a-sudden "ghost town" up in Iqaluit . . . and I don't know. Did I mention we were down to thirty students in one of my classes? By the end of November. That was after starting with eighty in the fall. Thirty kids wrote the final exam. How does that even happen? How does any of this happen? The streets around here are quiet now. I mean, every once in a while, you see a crowd, but it's not like before.

I have my bags packed, Lowell. Just in case. I don't want to leave the city, but I've got my shit packed just in case I have to . . . in case I have to run. Like, run. Do you understand? I keep getting this strange feeling. Every once in a while I'll be walking down the street, things will get real quiet suddenly, and my skin will just crawl.

Okay, look. We're not doing the interview anymore, okay? You can talk now.

I mean, I explained the paradox, so now we can drop this, right?

What are you doing? That's my leg.

What do you want to do right now?

When I got your email last month. So random. There have been a bunch of times since Halifax where I wondered . . . or thought about, I guess. If we had . . . back in Halifax, what if I tried . . . what if we had . . .

You didn't know what to do with me in Halifax.

You seem different now. More . . . lean or something. Hungry.

I like your hand there. That feels nice.

Turn it off, first. Lowell. The recorder.

LOWELL: Okay.

JANUARY

1.

JANE, 26 (MONTREAL, QC)

Yeah, so what's the date? What's the . . . it's January fifteenth, almost two weeks since we did this last, and the reason it's me doing this . . . recording this . . .

The emergency broadcast came on, that's why. The emergency broadcast. Residents are advised to stay in their homes . . .

I'M MESSING AROUND WITH YOUR TAPE RECORDER, LOWELL! You hear me? I know you can hear me in there. I'm turning on your tape recorder and messing around with your tapes and reading your notebooks and everything, so you better come out of that room! Do you hear? COME OUT OF MY ROOM!

YOU'RE ACTING LIKE A COWARD!

Residents are advised to stay in their homes. Residents are advised to avoid travel unless absolutely necessary . . .

The sound it makes. The radio. If I turn it on, it's just that frequency . . . that terrible sound that gets into your ears . . . scratches your eardrums. Same thing on the television. Except with a just a few lines of warnings to read against a bright blue backdrop.

Residents are advised to stay in groups. For more information, contact Services Québec at 1-877, et cetera . . . so we tried calling the number, and it rang and it rang and then it hung up on us! So we tried calling again, and it did the same thing and . . .

And so then Lowell began to freak out, and I was just trying to calm him down and then . . . and then we got into the fight.

I want you to come back out and be with me!

Because he's afraid. Which is . . . I mean, I get it. I'm afraid. I'm terrified.

So. I had to turn off the television because of that fucking emergency noise. It's on every channel now except the fireplace channel, for some reason. So you can either sit in front of a relaxing fake goddamned fireplace right now or you can make your ears bleed watching all of these emergency channels. I guess I could put it on mute. I could just put it on mute, I guess.

I don't know if we're gonna be okay or what. We've got lots of food and the apartment is a secure building with lots of people around us.

But we don't even know what's going on right yet, so . . .

Lowell! Get out of my room!

Lowell?

He won't come out.

LOWELL!

This is how it's gonna be, huh?

This is us?

Is this us?

2.

JANE, 26 / WANDAFRASH, 32 (MONTREAL, QC)

JANE: Hello, again, it's me, again. Jane. Lowell still hasn't come out of my bedroom. Which means I slept on the couch last night, and I am super happy about that. And I've been listening to his tapes and . . . I'VE BEEN LISTENING TO YOUR TAPES, LOWELL! I KNOW ALL ABOUT VICKI IN SACKVILLE!

Anyway, I figured I'd keep documenting events and people for him, because I am pretty sure it bugs him. I know he can hear me doing it. And I know it bugs him. It also gives me something to do while I try and distract myself from thinking about how pissed off I am at him because I had to SLEEP ON THE COUCH LAST NIGHT!

And so today, we have a very special guest with us. His name's Wandafrash, and he lives in the apartment across the hall from us in my building. Wandafrash? Would you like to say hello?

WANDAFRASH: Hello.

JANE: And Wandafrash, would you like to say anything about yourself?

WANDAFRASH: My name is Wandafrash. I live in the building.

JANE: And Wandafrash, I was wondering if you could talk about what's happening in the building today.

WANDAFRASH: What is happening?

JANE: Just . . . everything that's going on in the building right now.

WANDAFRASH: Yes. We are organizing a duty, a guard duty with the other residents.

JANE: What do you mean by guard duty?

WANDAFRASH: There will be two of us, tenants, in the lobby. To allow entrances and exits. There will be one of us, sitting, at the end of each hallway on every floor.

JANE: And how many floors are there in this building?

WANDAFRASH: In this building, there are twelve.

JANE: And so all of the tenants have decided to patrol the building.

WANDAFRASH: Yes, we will be working in shifts and watching. Watching the building for anything not right.

JANE: And how long will you be watching the building?

WANDAFRASH: Always.

JANE: Always.

WANDAFRASH: We will be watching in shifts. All of the tenants they have signed up for this—

JANE: Except for Lowell, because he locked himself in my bedroom.

WANDAFRASH: No, even he is on the list.

JANE: Even Lowell is on the list. Is everyone in the building on the list?

WANDAFRASH: Everyone in the building. We need everyone to be watching.

JANE: And what are we watching for?

WANDAFRASH: We do not know.

JANE: We have no idea, right?

WANDAFRASH: We do not know. But when people go missing . . . we do not want this happening here. No more.

JANE: Have people gone missing from the building?

WANDAFRASH: People have gone missing, yes.

JANE: From our building?

WANDAFRASH: Yes.

JANE: Who's gone missing?

WANDAFRASH: On the floors, the highest floors up, on every floor, people are going missing. So we need to be watching.

JANE: Do you think the building is safe, now, with everyone taking shifts and patrolling?

WANDAFRASH: No. The building is not safe.

JANE: You think the building isn't safe.

WANDAFRASH: This building is not safe.

JANE: Should we move out of the building?

WANDAFRASH: The government says no.

JANE: But do you think we should move out of the building?

WANDAFRASH: Where do we go? It is not just happening here. It is happening all over the city. It is everywhere.

JANE: So nowhere's safe.

WANDAFRASH: Nowhere is safe, I do not think this, no. But with many eyes, it is better.

JANE: This is why you've started the patrol shifts.

WANDAFRASH: If all of the tenants are watching, it will be impossible for as many people to go missing. If they do go missing, someone will see them go.

JANE: Why do you think people are going missing?

WANDAFRASH: I do not know. In my country, I am a refugee to Canada. In my country, people they have sometimes gone missing. But when people in my country have gone missing? You always knew who took them. If soldiers took them or if terrorists took them. Here you do not know why the people go missing.

JANE: The Canadian government says they think it's a terrorist organization.

WANDAFRASH: Eh? No. This is not the work of terrorists.

JANE: You don't think so, either?

WANDAFRASH: This is not the work of terrorists, no. I believe it is something else.

JANE: Why are people going missing, then?

WANDAFRASH: I do not know.

JANE: Why do you think people are going missing?

WANDAFRASH: I do not know.

JANE: When is Lowell supposed to go on patrol duty?

WANDAFRASH: He is scheduled for the lobby at eight p.m.

JANE: Then I need to make sure he is there.

WANDAFRASH: Yes, make sure he is there because we need many eyes to keep people from going missing.

JANE: Right. I will make sure he gets there. I'll get him out of my room.

WANDAFRASH: Thank you for this.

JANE: Do you have anything else you'd like to say before I turn off the tape recorder?

WANDAFRASH: No.

JANE: Would you like to help me break down a door?

WANDAFRASH: Yes. It will be fun.

3.

HOLLIS, 64 (MONTREAL, QC)

So we're out here in the lobby, like this. Two nights ago. Around three a.m. And I'm actually on lobby duty with Wandafrash because he's filling in for some girl named Maya because she didn't show up for her shift. And Wandafrash is looking overtired, because I think he's been trying to fill in a lot of the gaps in the shifts, to be honest. Because these shifts aren't the most fun of things, eh? You know what I mean, what is this, like your fourth or fifth, so far? So you know what I'm talking about. And I kind of understand why some people aren't showing up for their shifts, too. We're lucky tonight to get the lobby. But have you worked floor twelve yet? Floor twelve is so goddamned spooky. Worked the early morning up there last week and . . . just spooky, right? You're just watching this hallway, but you know the apartments behind most of the doors up there are empty because you've heard the stories about the higher up you go here and . . . I've never worked in a morgue, but the early morning shift up there, all by yourself. I bet that's the same feeling you'd have if you were a security guard in a morgue, I bet.

Security guard in a morgue.

So we're out here in the lobby two nights ago, Wandafrash and me, and Wandafrash, well, he starts kind of nodding off around the two thirty a.m. mark, and I kind of just let him drift off in his chair, you know? Because clearly the guy's been patrollin' extra shifts and needs the shut-eye.

And around three a.m., that's when the snow starts coming down, all soft and peaceful like. And I kind of just sit there for about twenty minutes or so, just watching everything outside get gradually blanketed by the stuff. And I think for the first time since they aired that press conference with the president and prime minister a couple of days ago I'm kind of feeling almost kind of at peace. Watching the snow fall. Everything quiet outside. The red neon of the cross on the hill shining off in the distance. I feel like one of those yoga guys pulling a downward dog or something. Like, Zen.

And then these flashes of light start happening. Like purple explosions of light in the building across the street. Right over there. On, like, their third and fourth floors. These all-of-a-sudden flashes of purple light. All over the place. Through the windows. Like if the building was a checkerboard and different squares were lighting up at a time. And quick, too. Like, flash-flash-flash! Like that. Different windows. And I guess the snow falling had kind of lulled me into a bit of a trance because I didn't react or anything to the flashes, at first. I didn't wake up Wandafrash or anything. I just kind of watched them. The flashes. Checkerboarding themselves across the surface of the building across the street.

Then the sounds of sirens. Drawing closer and closer, and the next thing I knew, there were cops and firefighters and a tank and the friggin' National Guard all congregated outside and storming their way into the building. Wandafrash, he woke up and next thing, this soldier is standing in front of the lobby door, knocking on it for us to let him in.

So we let him in, and he starts asking us about whether or not we saw anything and all like that. So I told him about the lights. The checkerboard of the lights through the windows that I saw. The purpleness of everything. And then he asked us what we were doing, and so Wandafrash told him about all of our shifts and patrol work and how we're working together in the building to watch everything. And he told us it was probably a good idea, to have everyone watching in shifts like we've been doing, and so then Wandafrash starts asking the military guy questions. And asking him what's happening and everything like that. And the military guy, he looks at me and Wandafrash, and he says:

"You know what an Etch A Sketch is?"

And Wandafrash has no idea what he's talking about, but I tell the guy, yeah, I know what an Etch A Sketch is.

"Well, that's what's happening. Except it's happening to us."

And then he told us to keep lockin' the doors at night and to keep doing what we're doing, and good job, citizens, and all like that.

And all of them, the cop cars, the fire trucks, the tank, the whole works, they were out of there and gone in less than an hour.

By now, it was around four thirty a.m. or so.

And it was still dark.

And it was still snowing. Snow blanketing the street again.

And Wandafrash told me not to let him fall asleep again. But he fell asleep again, like five minutes after that. And I just let him. Because the guy needed the rest.

A lot of action for a Tuesday night, eh? Or a Wednesday morning, whatever.

This happened right across the street. That building that we're watching right now. The other side of that glass.

I never told the wife about it. Edith. She's still not doing the best. Her nerves. And I mean, I'm still kind of processing it myself. Whatever it was that happened.

So what about you, anyway? Is Jane your girlfriend?

4.

JANE, 26 (MONTREAL, QC)

Lowell is recording me right now because it's been more than a week, and there hasn't been another press conference like they said there would be. So Lowell and I decided we should do another one of these recordings just to get our minds off of everything, just to break up the waiting around.

There was a man who was supposed to show up for his security shift this morning and relieve me. I was watching the second floor. He never showed up, so we got Wandafrash to track down the guy, and apparently, the guy, well . . . he's not around anymore, either. Either he left or . . . whatever it is that's happening, happened to him. Wandafrash was pretty upset because he said he had been talking with the guy just yesterday, and the guy said he'd report for duty. All of this trying to make sure the patrols are happening and people are relieving each other is really taking a toll on him, Wandafrash. He's looking pretty ragged.

In the daytime, I mean, we've gone outside a bunch. But there's not really a lot to do outside. On Sunday, we took a walk downtown. There were lots of people down there, Saint Catharine. Wandering around like us. They were holding some kind of vigil down there. The street was barricaded, and there was some kind of group parade thing, with people carrying torches. A memorial parade of some sort, for the vanished, I guess. Lowell and I walked right through the middle of it. They must have been burning incense, and you could smell whatever incense they were burning, and lots of people must have been smoking pot, you could smell weed everywhere, and I don't know. Lots of police around, watching everyone.

We walked right through all of that. Through that and through Chinatown and down to the old city. A lot of the roads down there hadn't even been plowed. Most of the shops and restaurants there were closed. We found one restaurant down there still open, so we went inside. It was almost empty, though. A group of seniors over in the corner, but other than them, it was just us. We sat down, there were these two men, in their fifties, all dressed to the nines. Amazing service, they gave us. Very classy. Like, professional waiters. And we asked them for menus and, they said, "No menus, today. What would you like?"

Lowell ordered a hamburger, and I had a club sandwich. And it was a really great club sandwich. Lowell loved his burger. It was a double burger. With brie and bacon and caramelized onions and . . . and I got out my purse to pay, and they just stared at us. Like we were crazy people. For trying to pay them. They wouldn't accept our money. "You don't understand," they said. "We are here until the end."

And so we walked back to the building here after that.

Sat around for a while. Played some cards. Had sex twice.

Just waiting for another press conference, now.

The phone lines don't work in the building now. The radio . . . there's no news on the radio anymore. The stations that are still broadcasting are either broadcasting pre-recorded stuff or emergency information. Everything you hear on the radio just loops. Or it is old content. Like *Dead Dog Café*. Same with the television. They were doing short news updates at about eleven p.m. at night there for a while on the CBC, but they haven't done that the past two nights. They just played some old French movies with subtitles and *King of Kensington* episodes.

There's no new material. No new information. Like the media is dying.

No one in the building has Internet anymore. People in the building are freaking out. I mean, they were freaking out before but no Internet kind of really started everyone . . .

One girl, Judy, we think her name was, went up to the roof and threw herself off . . .

We could try going to Toronto.

At least Lowell is feeling better now. He's looking better. Looking right at me.

He's all furry.

I love you, Lowell.

I said, I love you.

I figured it out when we were walking downtown. The way you held my hand. The way your hair kind of rustled when we walked. Your eyes, when you looked at me on the corner of Saint Catherine and Saint Denis.

You can respond to me now, you know. It's okay to respond.

He's nervous.

I love you.

He won't say it back. He won't say it back with the recorder on. He's shaking his head now. He wishes I wouldn't put him on the spot like this. I'm messing this up for him.

I love you, Lowell.

I do.

5.

WANDAFRASH, 32 (MONTREAL, QC)

I am Wandafrash. And everyone else, they are leaving.

I do not know anymore which ones have left and which ones are going missing. The ones that leave, they do not tell me, so I do not know. And now you are leaving, too. At least you let me know before you leave. You do not just run out of here.

The schedule did not work. People would not always show up. And then more people went missing. And then last night, someone went missing, on their shift. On duty. Up on floor twelve. And when they heard this, the tenants who were still up there, they all packed up and left the building. They said we were crazy to be staying here.

And they told this to the other tenants, and now many people are leaving. People are afraid to patrol the halls because of the tenant who went missing on his shift. I am afraid, too.

It is okay, if you want to be leaving. If Jane wants to be leaving. It is okay. But me? I will be staying. I will be staying here. Because this building? This building is now my home. This is my home now. This was the first place . . . that has ever been my home. Always, my family and I, we were moving. Refugees. No country. No home.

When we finally made it into this place, it took twelve years. Twelve years for them to approve. My family were not criminals. Twelve years of interviews. And why? Why twelve years? What sort of documents take twelve years to complete? You could write the Bible in twelve years. And they have computers now, today? Twelve years. C'mon, man. You have got to be kidding me. Twelve years. Hah!

This place, this building, is the first place I have lived since I came to this country. Since I came to Canada. My apartment, that is my first home. Real home. With my own real things inside, and my wife inside, and my son inside. I am not leaving.

My apartment is my home. This building is my home.

Nowhere is safe from this. People must understand. Nowhere is safe from this. It is not terrorists. No one is claiming responsibility for this. People must understand this now. Nowhere is safe now.

If you are leaving, where are you going?

Where are you going to go now, if you are leaving?

You will be missed. I will miss you.

But I will not go with you.

6.

EDITH, 64 (MONTREAL, QC)

The snow outside coming down like this . . . me and Hollis would never be able to make it, I'm afraid. Hollis is having problems with his knees, his arthritis is getting worse, and just the thought of him going out there in that snow . . . no, I can't let him do that. I don't care if he has a problem with that or not.

She shakes you up, doesn't she? Jane.

I'm glad they brought everyone from the upper floors down to the lower ones. Hollis was one of the ones helping to barricade all the stairways leading up past the fifth floor. Then, they had to move everyone into the empty apartments down here. You two were lucky you didn't have to move. Wandafrash is lucky, too. I think we would have had to wrestle the man from his apartment if he had been higher up.

Here are our snowshoes. They're gifts. As a thank you for letting us move into your apartment. I mean, Jane's apartment, but you two are together, right? Not much gets by me anymore.

These snowshoes, now, they were a gift to us. Hollis and I. For our wedding. They were given to us by Hollis's dad. Which is why we've held onto them, kept them all these years.

You two remind me of us. Hollis and I. When we were . . . younger.

I hope you make it to Toronto. And I certainly hope they're doing better in Toronto than we're doing here.

There is some advice I want to give you. First . . . stay together. You're stronger together than you are apart, even if you feel like screaming at each other over the little things. You're stronger together than you are apart.

Be smart about things and be smart about people. Every decision you make from here on out is going to count. There are no small decisions in life, so be smart about things, and be smart about people.

Stay warm, stay dry. Always eat a good breakfast. Eat a good breakfast because every day will always be uncertain. How a day is going to turn out, you never know what is going to happen. Chances are, you'll need your energy.

Maybe this will all be over before you get there, you know? Maybe the soldiers and the government will get to the bottom of this and fix it by then. Our grandchildren live in Calgary. I would very much like to see them again before the spring.

When Hollis and Wandafrash get back from their watch, we'll have one last big meal together. How does that sound? Bagels and squeaky cheese and pickles and smoked meat sandwiches and baklava.

You can still change your mind, too. Before the morning. If you want to stay. We're not so bad off here. I mean, I know things look bleak, but . . . at least we're looking out for each other here.

It's going to be a cold, long road for you two, if you really do leave tomorrow.

But I think you can make it. You'll make it.

You remind me of Hollis and I. When we were . . .

We didn't really know what we were doing either.

We just kind of went for it, you know?

And now here we are.

We made it this far.

LOWELL (HIGHWAY 401, ON)

We're on the 401 somewhere . . . near the Quebec border somewhere . . . I don't know . . .

There's this idea of fate, or something. That you can kind of
get . . . stuck in your head. Like, things are meant to be a certain
way, because of this thing that happened or that thing that happened. You take things as signs. You construct this narrative, and
then everything you see after that, you kind of see it as part of your
fate, or your story or your . . .

We have a fate. Together. We have a . . . FATE!

WE HAVE A FATE, YOU FUCKING . . . YOU FUCKING . . . WE HAVE A . . .

So . . . that's how I . . . that's how I know . . . how I know she'll
be back. Anytime now.

Even though she left an hour ago.

Even though I let the stupid fire burn out when I left to go looking for her.

Even though I followed her tracks, and her tracks just stop
right over there. Right by the fucking . . . the fucking . . . forest . . .
forest . . . line . . .

She's coming back.

She's coming . . . JANE!

Because it's fate.

Fuck, what the fuck . . . what the fucking fuck . . . WHAT THE
FUCK AM I DOING HERE?

THIS IS FUCKING BULLSHIT!

JANE!

JANE!

It's . . . freezing . . . and it's . . . it's freezing . . .

JANE!

She's my . . . she's my big noise . . .

FEBRUARY

1.

TODD, 28 (LANCASTER, ON)

Things are really going to shit, aren't they? Things are really going to shit. We thought things were going to shit before, but ... naw ... now they're really going to shit. Things are really going to shit, now, man. When you gotta send home electricians to jerry-rig a village's electricity just to keep the fuckin' lights on and refrigerators running, well, I mean, that's a sign right there, you know?

When you gotta hole up in a pub with all these other wingnuts and assorted people because you're afraid because your house is on the outskirts, and you're afraid of living on the outskirts because who the fuck knows when you'll go missing too or get abducted by aliens or terrorists or whatever the fuck is going on ... and this is Canada, man. We used to eat doughnuts here.

They only got two constables left in town. And they got into a fistfight, right here on the main drag here, right in plain view of everyone, in the middle of the day, the last two cops in town just dukin' it out. Dukin' it out for everyone to see. And then the fight, it didn't even end up with one of them or the other getting knocked out or hurt or anything like that. The fight, it ended with the two cops, they started hugging each other, crying in each other's arms. That's how crazy everything has gotten. Again, right in plain view. These two cops who'd been dukin' it out were crying and hugging right here on the main drag in the middle of the day for everyone to see. And lots of people were watchin', too. Because it's not like any of us have been able to watch TV since the networks went down. So what else are you gonna do, except watch the two remaining neighbourhood cops whale on each other and sort out their personal affairs in the street?

My ex, she used to give me all of this shit about hanging out here too much. The pub. And so I'd try not to go here as often. But now here I am holing up inside of it with all of these other whack jobs. Things are really going to shit is what I'm trying to say.

That's my opinion. Of things. For your documentary? Whatever it is you're doing.

You see, my dad sold the family land because he wasn't getting enough from his pension to get by. Just to survive. That's how well the government was looking after him with the pension money. So Dad sold the land, there was nothin' for me to inherit here. I had to start my own business, shoe repair business, make my own way in the world. I never had no intentions of moving away from Lancaster, I grew up here, had to do something with myself, though, because it's not like my dad could bail me out of any of the sticky situations life throws at ya on a regular basis.

Your boots, by the way. The zipper on that left boot of yours, I can fix that if ya want. That's fixable. We could walk over to the shop; it's just two buildings up the road here. I got the gear, we can fix that. Re-stitch that bookbag of yours, maybe, too. If you're stickin' around for a bit.

It looks like you probably should stick around for a bit, too. At least a couple of days, anyway. You look like shit. You look like a cow patty someone stepped in. What'd you fall on your face or something? Maybe Carly can get you some peroxide or Polysporin on some of those cuts. Carly's all right. She owns the place. You've probably already met her, though, I imagine.

Anyway, yeah, I can fix your boots. You must have been out there for a while, eh? On the road. Cold out there, right now. It was what, thirty below last night?

Probably a miracle you even made it here from Montreal.

We don't go anywhere outside of the pub unless we're in groups. We are firm believers in the buddy system around here. The electricians, the repair team, they all drive around in the same van. No one lets anyone out of their sights. We buddy up to go to the john. Even with us all in the pub here. Because believe it or not, we have lost people before, not here in the pub. We have lost people on fucking bathroom breaks before. Not me, personally. I haven't lost track of my buddies yet. I haven't seen it happen. But a couple people have.

I remember I used to watch those post-apocalyptic-type shows on TV. You know, the ones with the zombies takin' over the Earth or aliens invading the planet, those kinds of shows. How those shows were always so action-packed, and there were monsters, actual monsters that you could see and fight and . . . so I carry a gun on me, right? Because things have gone so to shit that it's starting to feel like we might be stuck in some kind of scenario like one of those shows. Except for no one's seen anything. When I say people have seen their buddies go missing, what I mean is, they haven't actually seen their buddies go missing. Their buddies have just gone missing out of frame, if you understand what I mean. If what's happening to us were a TV show, everything crazy is happening outside of the frame, you know? Like a low-budget TV show that can't show you anything because they didn't have the money for the special effects. No one's seen any monsters. Or terrorists. Or anything. So I carry a gun now, but I mean, most of the time . . . I mean, I don't even know what I'm carrying a gun for, you know? The whole thing, everything . . . it's confusing the shit out of me, more than anything else. I might as well be carrying a book of how to solve Sudoku puzzles as carrying around a gun because no one even knows what the threat is. We just know the symptoms of it.

It's just a matter of what type of glue you use. On a zipper like that. We got some good-quality glue here. I got some down in my shop. We'll go tomorrow. It'll keep those boots together for another year, you mark my words. I know what I'm doing.

But things are really going to shit, aren't they?

2.

ED, 42 (LANCASTER, ON)

You ever hear of that term "bangers and mash"? It's a pub dish. Sausages and potatoes. Sausages are the bangers, and the mash refers to everything else on the plate besides the sausages. Well, a friend of mine has a saying. Or he did, back when he was still around. "You can't banger without the mash." You get it? You can't . . . you know . . . without being left with everything else on the plate. You get it?

Half of 'em here, these people, we're all hunkered down with, they got this belief in people, in humanity, like together, we can get through this thing or whatever. And then someone goes missing. And then there's all of this wailing and crisis and crying and tragedy and faith being tested and all of that shit.

I don't believe in any of this. Any of this shit they're doing here. I'm just hunkering down here because it's relatively safe at the moment. I don't talk to any of them if I don't have to. Hell, the only reason I'm talking to you is to save you from becoming like them. Believe in the strength of people working together or whatever the fuck.

You can't banger without the mash. You get me? My buddy had it right. I mean, he was talking about chicks at the time, but it holds true with everyone. You can't hit the sweet spot with people and not expect all of this shit to come with it. You can't make a friend without all of the baggage they bring to the friendship.

And I can tell, I can see it in your fuckin' eyes. You know what I am talking about. You've just gone through something like this. You got involved with someone, didn't you? You did. I can tell. And all of the mash that came with it. And now you're a fucking mess inside, aren't ya? And you could have avoided it all if you had just stuck to yourself.

This place is safe now, but it won't be for long. I don't think so. I don't believe that. What's to stop this little pocket of humanity from crumbling when everywhere else is falling apart? We don't even know what's happening in the cities right now.

Do you have a gun yet? Do you want one? Because I have one I can give you. I'll have to show you how to use it first. So you don't blow your own goddamned foot off, but I have a gun I can give you. And you can have it. And two clips of ammo for it. And I'll show you how to use it. Because I can tell you just been through something. And I feel . . . I shouldn't feel anything at all, shouldn't let myself feel anything at all, but I do. I feel like you're some kind of kid that just got caught up in some kind of mistake. Mistakes happen. To all of us. We all make mistakes. I sure did. My buddy, my buddy I was telling you about, who said that about the bangers and mash, we were pretty tight. Saw the world in pretty much the same way. We were out hunting when he disappeared. This was in the early days of all of this. Back in October. No one knew it was going to be this big thing or anything like that back then. We were hunting partridge. He took the ridge. I took the dell. I returned from the dell. He never returned from the ridge. And we'd been hunting that land since we were ten years old. Since before we were even legally allowed to shoot guns. His name was Jake. He was my best friend. Good enough that I had never needed another. And then came the mash. You know what I mean? I was living like a ghost right up until that press conference snapped me back into survivor mode. We all make mistakes.

I'll help you get back on your feet. You learn how to use my gun, you'll be able to defend yourself. That's a good thing. But don't expect us to become friends or anything. I'll help you get back on your feet, but you gotta learn how to stand up for yourself.

No matter what, do not befriend these people. And don't try and befriend me. Do yourself a favour.

I don't think this place will survive the winter.

You'll be lucky if you do.

3.

CARLY, 37 (LANCASTER, ON)

My name is Carly Wilson, and I am the current owner of the Stone Circle Pub, here in the beautiful splendour that is Lancaster, Ontario. I am thirty-seven years old. I am a Pisces. Which is some kind of fish, I've been told. I don't know what kind of fish it is, but it's some kind of fish. Don't know if it's a trout or salmon or something out of the ocean like a bluefin tuna. What else do you want to know about me?

The bar's been in the family for two generations now, and I've been running the place for my father ever since he disappeared in July. And since my mom and sister went missing in November, I've opened this place up kind of like a refuge for people who don't feel safe living alone. I made sure that we were good and stocked with food and alcohol enough for the winter, but I wasn't sure how bad everything was gonna get, so now here we are, middle of February and I'm starting to wonder if the stores are going to last until spring or not. We burned through all of the good Scotches and rum last month, but we have tons of beer left. The one smart thing Dad did was install an extra-large beer fridge in the basement. I was able to make sure we were super stocked with the stuff before everything started really going south.

I don't mind having a drink, either. And if this turns out to be the end of the world or something crazy like that, then you, me, none of us should be afraid of getting drunk. As much as humanly possible. Can you imagine, coming around to the end of it all, the end of days, and having all of this unused liquor still hanging around? Bet you we'd all feel some stupid then.

More than anything, I'm keeping the place open like this to calm people's nerves. The ones that are left. Around three weeks ago, I started the whole community wake session. So that, every Friday, anyone who was interested can come here and drink their fill. And we get Harvey over there, Harvey, he's the town mayor—he rattles off the list of people we've lost each week. And then after he's done reading off the list of names, Paul and Emily over there, Paul, he's a fiddler and Emily she can sing pretty decent, so we get Paul to start playing his fiddle and Emily sings along. All of the old songs. Irish stuff. Gaelic stuff. Scottish songs and all that. It kind of becomes like an old-fashioned Irish Rovers's pub party after that point. You remember that? The Irish Rovers, how they used to have that show on TV? And it was basically like a big pub party that you could watch on TV. My mother and I used to watch it. That was before we had cable, so there was nothing else on, right? I was just a little kid. But I liked it. Because I knew Dad was here, when I was watching the show, I knew my dad was working in the bar here doing the same thing as what we were doing—watching TV. So I always liked that show.

You caught me at kind of the sweet spot. I'm about three beers into my evening, here. Probably in the perfect state. I don't mind talking right now, like this. I could probably fill that tape recorder of yours, if you let me keep going. Not about anything in particular. I don't really have anything in particular to say about anything, really. Plus, I'm busy enough just keeping all of this going around us. The repair crew, they're gonna be walking in here soon. Half of them are sleeping here now. Most of the rest of them are set up in the fire hall down the street there. Gary's sleeping across the road in the convenience store with the Smiths and the Gundersons. Anyway, I got people to look after, I guess is what I'm saying. So it's not like I don't have anything to do.

Your cuts are healing up okay, though. That's good to know. At least nothing got infected.

You put any more thought into helping the constables out with their night patrols? I don't think they've had many other people expressing much interest. Not since that last storm. It's too fucking cold out, now, for most people. Nearly froze my tits off today, running from here across the street to pick up condiments from the store. It's like the snow came last to us this year, but when it came, it really fuckin' came, you know what I mean? And it brought the cold with it.

I'm surprised they were able to repair that transformer that blew last week. And we're lucky it was the only thing that blew up with these temperatures.

My beer's getting pretty low. You want another? I'm going to have another. Fuck, it's only six thirty. Lots of night left to get through. We still got the long stretch to come. Yes, we still got the long stretch ahead of us.

I kind of like it, here. Like, being here. Like this. I kind of am really proud of myself. I'm proud I stocked up before the winter. That I can provide this to people. This place. Where we can read the names and still sing songs and have music and warm people up and feed people and everything.

My dad didn't really want me working here, I don't think, growing up. I insisted, when I came back from college, and I bugged him enough, finally he had to give in, right? Because where the hell else was I going to work in Lancaster? But I don't think he ever intended me working here.

But I think he'd be proud of me now. Really, I do. Wherever he is. Wherever he went.

He'd be proud. I'm sure of it. He'd be proud of me.

I'm going to have another. You want another?

4.

CONSTABLE XAVIER, 39 (LANCASTER, ON)

He damn near broke my jaw, and I think he knew that at the time, and that's ultimately what made us pause the fight, if you ask me. He clocked me. Connected, too, in just the right place, and my jaw it popped. Made this big sound. We both thought at first it might be broken. It wasn't, though. Which was lucky as hell for me. Well, for both of us, really. Because we were pissed at each other, but it's not like we wanted to kill each other or anything. We just had to get it out of our system, you know?

Because when things started going downhill, it started this rift, eh? Half of us were really skeptical and concerned with what everything CSIS, and then the government and eventually the military, what they were telling us. Those guys in the black suits with the teeth. What they were telling us to do. Half of us were skeptical, but the other half of us were just trying to do what we were told by the higher-ups, so . . . that's how the rift started. And George, he had just been trying to follow orders like he was supposed to throughout the whole thing. But me and some of the other fellas, well, we were skeptical, all the way back when they started telling us we had to keep checking in with the media, make sure those idiots understood they couldn't just go reporting every disappearance all willy-nilly and starting a panic in the people. I mean, the police keeping your media quiet, that's like something you see in other countries, really. On this kind of scale, I mean. On the type of scale they were asking from us this time around.

So some of us were starting to get really cynical about things, and started sharing whatever information we could with the media to hopefully help them get the message out so people would know what was going on and wouldn't be so vulnerable to whatever it was that was happening. Because we're just a provincial force, we're not the RCMP, and we, you know, meet a lot of the people that we're policing face to face and all like that.

But some of the guys, like George, who were just following orders, well they heard about some of the rest of us sharing information and all of that, and that pissed them all off.

And meanwhile this great vanishing of people was happening everywhere. Of course we knew about it. You know how many missing persons reports I have personally, I mean, personally handled the paperwork for? We knew about all of it since September. And there was evidence it started happening before September even. Probably back as early as June, I think. But CSIS, the government, the guys in the black suits, they wanted everything to be kept as hush-hush as possible until they could figure out how to spin it. How to get all of the information under control and spin it so that people wouldn't, I don't know, revolt or whatever. Get rowdy. Because people are rowdy. Especially in groups, they get rowdy. I mean, people are rowdy by nature, but put them in a group, right?

So there had been this rift brewing between all of us. At the detachment. And all of this vanishing of people happening around us. And then some of our own started going missing. Not reporting in for shifts and all of that. Which stretched all of us out. We started working extra shifts. On top of all the regular shit which we had to police. Like the domestics and people just getting up to their usual stupid shenanigans. And this just kept getting worse and worse. People I'd worked beside for years just all of a sudden not showing up for work, and then I never saw them again. Same thing as George was going through. And the government just kept telling us to hold the line, keep things contained, and all like that.

And I'll always remember, this was a month ago, I came into work, and George was standing in the chief's office. Just standing there, staring at the chief's chair. Office was empty except for me and him.

It just had kind of happened all around us, eh? We'd gotten to the point we were so tired and overworked and trying to hold the line and—

George kind of blamed me and the others for not holding the line, earlier on, you know? And I kind of blamed him for putting his orders before the people here. Even though we were both on the same side. The whole time. We'd been on the same side.

We were just walking across the street together, walking side by side, and I was exhausted. We were heading across the street toward our patrol car, and I don't know what it was, I just had some kind of emotion just all of a sudden kind of rise up inside of me. And I just turned and hit him. Mid-stride. And I just kind of looked at him after I hit him, I don't know if I expected him to fall or what. I didn't intend to hit him more than once. But I had to hit him that one time for some reason.

And then, he was on me. Just rapid fire . . . pow-pow-pow, pummelling the shit out of me and then he pulled his fist way back and just launched one right onto my jaw. And so then . . . the sound my jaw made. We thought he had broken it.

On top of everything, standing in the middle of this town we couldn't protect, that was falling apart, on top of all that, we thought he had broken my jaw. And he looked at me. And I touched my jaw with my hand. And I could tell it was still in one piece. Still connected to the rest of me. Just a close call, was all it was. And I let out this kind of, oh, I don't know, sigh of relief, I guess I must have. And after I sighed, that's when I started crying. Because it had been such a close call. I mean, can you imagine a broken jaw on top of everything else?

And he saw me crying and . . . he realized he didn't hate me or anything, he wasn't really angry at me, not even for hitting him . . . he was more angry about the town falling to shit on our watch and so . . . well, yeah, he started crying, too. And then he hugged me. And I guess that's the story behind all of that. And I mean, people were watching us as all of this happened. I imagine there's been gossip.

But, I mean, let's face it. When you're a cop, you know people are gonna gossip about ya. We're aware of the rifts around us. It's not like *they're* invisible.

5.

EMILY, 41 (LANCASTER, ON)

Paul, I think Paul might be in love with me. Which is really sweet. He's very sweet and honest and naïve . . . I mean, fuck. But that's just who he is. And there's nothing wrong with that. But he's representative of that type, if you follow me, because there are two types. There's the type that believe in the razzle-dazzle of it all, and then there's the type who understand that the razzle-dazzle of it all . . . it's just a singer trying to make her way, if you follow.

It's an act. Of course it's an act. I know that. Paul thinks he knows that, and so he plays along, he even promotes the show. He'll set up in the corner, all innocent and matter of fact, and just start tuning his fiddle. Applying resin to the bow. No one else in the place suspects, at that point, that he's about to launch into a performance. That the way the whole gig works is that Paul starts off by Paul not intending to play. He's just performing maintenance on his violin.

And then, once he's tuned, he plays a few notes from some crowd pleaser. A few notes from "Rattlin' Bog," or "Black Velvet Band." He plays a few notes, and then he stops and listens. He listens to the room. And what's he listening for? He's listening to see if he can hear anyone, humming or singing or whistling . . . he's listening to see if someone in the room picked up the song. Because if someone in the room has picked up the song, like, in their head, and they might not even be aware that they've done it, but what it means is that person's ready to sing along. And if someone in the room is ready to sing along, that means someone in the room's ready to listen. Which means, all of a sudden, we have an audience. Which means, all of a sudden we got someone ready to buy into the act. And if he hears someone start to pick up a song, that's when he'll launch into a little more of it. He'll play a couple of phrases, and make it look like he's just messing around a bit with his fiddle. Like, casually. He's still coming off as though he has no intention of performing. And he never plays the full chorus at this point. That's a rule.

By this point, however, whomever it is that has picked up the song, they want to, really want to hear the song, by this point. And this is when they usually speak up. Paul will stop playing the song right before the chorus of the thing, and someone in the all-of-a-sudden audience we've so subtly built will say something. Something like "Awww . . . " or "Play it!" or "Play the whole thing!"

And that's when we know the hustle is gonna work big time. You make them ask for it. First, you make them think it was their idea in the first place. Then, you make them ask for it. Once they ask for it, the song, you give them what they ask for. You give them what they didn't even know they wanted in the first place. And Paul will start playing the song. He'll even play the chorus. And then, halfway through the second verse, I'll finally take notice of him. Because I've been drinking at the bar this whole time. In my dress. Looking exhausted. Or trying to keep to myself. But I let myself overhear the performance. I let myself notice the song. And I let everyone see how I just can't help myself. How I just can't help but fall under the spell of Paul and his fiddle. Everyone in the audience gets to watch me, out of the corner of their eye, they get to watch me go through what they just went through.

The final stage, Paul and I, after Paul has already given them what they wanted, we take it one step further. We give them something they never even imagined would happen. I start singing. From my seat at the bar. And when I start to sing, people get excited, because it's fun, another person joining the game. But when I sing, I reveal my talent. My voice. And I really let it out, really let them have it. Everyone. And Paul gets this look in his eyes, one of surprise. As though he didn't expect me to blow everyone away with my voice, if you follow me.

After the show, and we perform until we feel tired, that's pretty normal for us . . . after the show, I go back to my seat at the bar. And then I wait. Takes about a minute or less. Someone always comes over. Here, in this place, it's either Carly, or one of the guys from the repair crew, or sometimes Paul himself. And I got nothing to worry about for the rest of the evening. All the food and drink and pot and places to sleep I can handle.

Before this whole state-of-emergency stuff I never lacked for anything. If you can sing, if you understand the steps of how the hustle works, you don't have to worry about a single damn thing. You can make yourself the queen of a different little shithole every night of the week.

But like I said, there are two types of people in the world. People who know what the razzle-dazzle really is, and then . . . well, the people who actually believe in it. Like, fully, with their whole hearts and souls and . . . even though the illusion . . . it's an economy, you follow me? It's just an economy. People working to survive.

So I don't buy into this place, either, as a result. This bar. Lancaster. What these people are all trying to do here by keeping themselves all together. Lancaster isn't some kind of special little place or special group of people. They're not some kind of family or anything like that. This is just another shitty dive with a bunch of losers crammed into it . . . trying to convince themselves that life right now isn't as shitty as it really is. A bunch of terrified losers getting more lonely and insane, night by night. They turn into junkies. Junkies for here. This moment in time. Junkies for the memory of an illusion. Something that didn't exist in the first place. They turn from junkies into living ghosts, and then eventually they'll all just disappear altogether.

I get the hustle. I been doing it my whole life, this act. This bar is just like all of the others. I shake my hips. I breathe out when I sing. The world around me turns into a ghost, and I am always aware of the grave. How I am dancing and singing as I drift toward my inevitable fate, which can only be death. But the hustle is fun. The act is fun. I want to keep having fun. Until I end up in the ground. Or until Paul starts to get too creepy and asks me to do something gross like marry him.

Ugh. Marriage. Talk about illusions. Talk about people deluding themselves. I'd be happier in the dirt.

6.

CONSTABLE GEORGE, 44 (LANCASTER, ON)

No, I want you to record me, because I want ... we're getting to the point where me and Xavier have abandoned trying to fill out paperwork or anything like that. So there's not going to be any printed record of this, but that being said, I do believe there's something in what I'm about to tell you that I'd kind of like you to take away from this with you, okay?

First off, I ... me and Xavier, we really appreciate you volunteering to ... "help" ... us, with the patrols and everything. That's ... great, and everything. And I just want to say that you're really ... it's nice to see that initiative in someone your age ... and that you're ... enjoying your time here in Lancaster and everything. Carly says you've been helping her at the pub and that's great ... but in terms of helping us with the patrols ... well.

I'm just going to put it out there, first off. You don't have any training in law enforcement, first off. I mean, a bunch of security shifts in some apartment building that's great and all but it doesn't really mean you've had any real experience, first off. Just because you know how to use that gun of yours, first off, you're lucky I don't just take that gun from you so you don't hurt yourself. If circumstances were different right now, I'd just be taking that firearm from you, first off, okay?

The second thing is ... me and Xavier aren't really sure, right now, how much longer this place is going to last. If you get my meaning. We were talking about it last night and ... neither one of us really know what's going to happen next. I mean, we have some idea of what's going to happen, next, right? Someday soon here, the power is going to go off, and the repair teams aren't going to be able to get it going again. We're lucky that it's been starting to warm up early, because I don't think the power's going to last for much longer. I think once that power shuts off for good . . . I mean, some people are probably going to stay here. Some of the townies. The people in the pub. But once that power goes, a lot of the guys on the repair team, they're going to be leaving. They're going to be heading for somewhere they actually have a shot of fixing things up, if you know what I mean.

And me and Xavier aren't sure if we're going to keep enforcing the law so much after that, okay? We were talking about it last night. We're not sure if there's much point in . . . the whole . . . keeping-up-appearances thing so much anymore. If the power goes. If the repair guys leave.

And we sure the hell don't want set up some kind of patrol duty just to have everything fall to shit and then have to tell you we've decided to shut down the detachment, I guess, is what I'm saying. If you did something stupid, like try and stay behind after we leave and started thinking of yourself as like, I don't know . . . the sheriff or something here. Like you had some kind of legitimacy backing you up in that kind of instance. Because you're just a kid. First off.

A place like this isn't going to become your burden. If you get me. We're not going to let you think like you have the right to make this place your burden when you don't. You're not from here, and you seem like a real good kid so we're not going to allow that to happen. We don't want you getting any kind of crazy stupid ideas in your head.

But we get that you want to help. So what I want to offer you is a ride out of town. After we're done talking here. Me and Xavier need a couple of letters delivered to Gananoque. Apparently, the military have set up some kind of rally point in Gananoque. Why Gananoque? I have no idea. The place is a fucking tourist trap. It's not a defendable position or anything. Regardless, we need someone to deliver some information to them.

If you're up to doing that.

The people here don't need you to stay. We don't need you to stay here. You're not even from here. But we need to send word to Gananoque about what's happening here. And we think you could make it. If you're serious about helping us.

We lost two guys yesterday. From the repair team. Two of the more knowledgeable guys. I don't want to get into it, all I'm saying is . . . we're losing people here. People we need to keep this thing going.

I don't think that all of us gathering around each other is turning out to be the right move for us. For people, I mean. I just think it paints a brighter target on all our backs. Makes it easier for whomever it is that's doing this to find us.

Me and Xavier think you stand a better chance of making it on your own.

Follow the roads, but walk through the woods, you get me? Keep quiet. That sort of thing. Tell anyone you meet along the way to do the same.

You're gonna be like a modern-day Laura Secord. Think of it like that. Fun, yeah? You remember? Like from one of those Canadian Heritage Minutes?

You can make it to Gananoque, kid. I get that it's cold. But you can make it. Here are the letters.

MARCH

LOWELL (HIGHWAY 401, ON)

I've got frostbite on my ears right now because of the wind chill. I had to stop and set up camp and shake the snow out of my boots. Because when your boots get wet inside, in this weather, you can't ever seem to dry them out. And then your feet are always wet and freezing. I'm getting sick of eating canned food. Every night is either beans or pasta, corned beef hash. I'm getting sick of having to start my own campfire. Every time I get wet. But I don't want to build it too big. I have to try and keep it big enough to stay warm but small enough to keep a low profile. Pretty much everything sucks right now.

More weird dreams last night. Can't remember much of them except . . . I could hear someone screaming. In the dream . . . I could hear it. This screaming. And then I woke up in my lean-to next to my fire, and I thought I could still hear the screaming. Like, in reality. Just off in the distance. And I know this is wrong, but I thought the screaming, I thought it sounded like Jane. Thought I heard Jane screaming. Out in the darkness in the woods some-where. So I turned on the tape recorder to capture it. And then when I couldn't hear it anymore, I tried playing back what I had recorded. And there was nothing on the tape. No screaming. Because it hadn't really been there. Not really. It had just been in my head. Jane screaming. Because she exists only in my head now.

We were surfing, back in Lawrencetown. Me and Jane and JP and Connor. We were all, like, fourteen, fifteen years old, around that. Jane was sixteen.

And the surf was pretty okay that morning. You could grab a wave and just ride it for a long . . . a long time. Nothing crazy but . . . just this real nice steady surf. And we were all just kind of doing our thing. This ghost fog all around us.

And Jane just got up on her board this one wave . . . and she just rode it out. And I just kind of watched her ride it out. The whole way. And she looked . . . she looked like . . . it's kind of hard to describe what I was thinking when I was watching her, but I couldn't stop watching her, you know?

I was so distracted that I let go of my board. It floated out in front of me and I didn't even notice, I was too busy watching Jane . . . but my board it got kind of turned sideways, and the next wave came and it smashed my board into my head. And I don't know what happened next. Because it knocked me out.

But when I woke up, I was looking into her eyes. Jane's. And our eyes kind of . . . we looked right into each other.

JP and Connor were standing around. JP told me he thought I'd drowned. Connor thought I was dead. But Jane had resuscitated me.

When I opened my eyes, and we were looking into each other . . . it was one of those kind of moments. Like . . . the potential of a new life, sort of feeling. Like, fate.

There's so much stuff that exists only in my head now.

I need to find somebody. I need people.

I've seen people on the roads. There are people here and there, moving about. Trying to get God-knows-where.

Maybe if I find someone good heading my way, I might just see if I can join up with them. Share the road with somebody for a while.

I gotta get moving again. I have these letters to deliver from Lancaster, after all. Make sure I get them to Gananoque. These letters won't deliver themselves, right?

I think I can make it to Gananoque in a couple of days. If I keep pushing hard. I just gotta . . . keep pushing hard.

So, mush, husky. Mush. Mush.

1.

VIOLET, 76 (CORNWALL, ON)

It really hasn't been that much of a winter at all. No, it could have been a lot worse. That's for sure. I don't mind the snow, but I hate the cold. I don't like the wind. When it's cold and the wind picks up. I just get so cold now, even with my coat on and my scarf and mittens, it just gets so cold. But now, it's starting to melt you can tell. Now it's warming up. Not very much, but a bit. A little bit. That's why I was asking you to shut the door when you came in. I asked you to shut the door, and you just looked at me like a baby squirrel who's forgot where he buried an acorn. I had to tell you to shut the door! How long have you been out there, anyway? By yourself in the snow. You must have been freezing. We're lucky it hasn't really been much of a winter at all. No, it could have been a lot worse.

I love to talk to people. You're the first company I've had since last week when Father Yerxa came out to see me. Which was very nice of him. He didn't have to do that. But he did. Gave me the blessing. I was lucky I had some raspberry jam in the cellar, or I wouldn't have had anything to send him off with. He's a nice man.

I used to go to the service every Sunday morning with Alice, but she stopped showing up here a few weeks ago. She'd always pick me up in her Oldsmobile. We'd drive down together. Into the main part of town where the church is. Have you been in town yet? It's nice. The church is beautiful.

Alice would sing in the choir, she had a really nice voice. My voice can't hit the really high notes anymore, so I always sat in the congregation. The crowds were small enough I had my own pew all to myself. But I could see Alice from where I was sitting for the whole service. She was right in my main view. And every once and a while she'd catch my eye and wink at me, or whenever Father Yerxa would make a joke in the sermon or introducing the next hymn, we'd smile at each other. She was a very good singer. She even had her own band that used to play for her when we were both younger. A long time ago now. We were just kids. She had a band playing behind her, and they would play at the community hall and the arena every other weekend or so. They played all the new songs, even the ones our parents didn't want us listening to like "Rock Around the Clock" and all of those. All of the good ones.

After Rod died from that stroke . . . Rod was Alice's husband, and she swore she would never marry again. Me . . . I just never got married.

I just never had anyone who . . . ever wanted to ask.

And after every service, Alice and I would help the ushers collect the extra programs from the pews and tidy up. And then she'd drive me back to my house, here, and we'd always have Red Rose tea and biscuits. I'd make the biscuits the night before. Every Saturday night, during *Hockey Night in Canada*, while that was still on. I'd be cooking biscuits for Sunday brunch with Alice. She really liked biscuits, and we both liked our Red Rose tea.

And Father Yerxa noticed that we haven't been showing up to church lately. He's a very nice man. He filled up my woodbox before he left. All of my wood for the winter, I had the men pile it downstairs in my cellar. It's dry down there. I have to go downstairs whenever I need to fill my woodbox up by the stove. That stove's a great little stove. I boil my water on it and everything. I ordered it from Simpsons-Sears years back in the eighties.

I knew three weeks ago when it was time to go and her Oldsmobile never showed up. I figured they got her, now, too. She was my ride to church. She always came to pick me up.

Very nice of the man to come and visit me at home. He doesn't have to do that. If he comes back again, I have lots of raspberry jam in the cellar.

Could be worse. Yes, could be much worse. Hasn't been much of a winter at all, really. I think people got so used to everything being so convenient. Everything was getting so convenient. The snow, we'd get a snowstorm and the roads would be plowed before the next morning. The power would go out, and they'd have it back up and running in an hour or so. And people started carrying their phones around with them, everywhere they went. Everything was getting so convenient.

When I was growing up things weren't like that. You could get snowed in for weeks. You had to be prepared for a storm. You had to buy groceries in advance, and stock up on wood. You didn't know if they'd get the power going again or not. Just like it is now, I guess. Like we've gone back in time, almost.

Everything was getting so much better, it seemed. If you had been alive as long as I have. You would have known that. How everything was getting so much better. People were carrying their phones with them! Everywhere they went!

And then, of course, now, this happens. And poor Alice.

I imagine whoever they are will just bundle me up in a big sack and haul me out into the woods some night here soon, now. But you can't do anything about it. Whoever it is that's doing it, they're going to keep doing it until they get it out of their system. Whatever's bugging them. Whatever point they have to prove to themselves. It's a shame because everything was getting so much better.

Would you mind bringing me up a few armloads of wood from the cellar? If you could just fill my woodbox, that would be fine. That will keep me going for another couple of days.

It's a good stove. Ordered it from Sears.

2.

EM, 42 (BROCKVILLE, ON)

My name is Em, and this is hilarious. This is just funny. And you won't talk at all, that's the deal, huh? You'll just let me ramble on about anything I want to? So you can capture humanity. Capture humanity. Now that's a funny word. Capture. Funny. Did I mention I was a prison guard? At the jail over in Kingston. Back before the place caught on fire. Back before everyone left. Before I left. Before I came here. And then we have this fuckin' place. Brockville. You may not have noticed it yet, but the town here, pretty much everyone has left. Did you notice how quiet it is here, yet? I thought I might be the only one here in town. If there's anyone else, I haven't found them, yet. Most people tried to make their way to Toronto, I think. Most of them. Some might have been heading for Montreal. Some. But I think I might be the only one here. Walking the streets of Brockville. Em Murrell.

I don't mind leaving. Hitting the road again. Not at all. Need to go where the action is. It's boring here. I've been bored for days now. I had a little buddy; he helped me get here from Kingston. But I been a man alone since him and me parted ways.

It's fate, I guess, right? I'm getting bored, last man standing, and the universe sends you right to me. And my feet have been getting itchy, let me tell you. I have been getting restless.

We can get there on foot in a day. Keeping to the roads. But I don't think we should follow the road. Road's dangerous now. You seen the purple lights, yet?

They were here in town just last night. I saw them flashing in some of the houses just down the street here. Whatever they are.

Whoever they are. I could see them though the crack of the door of the house I was crashing in.

Only thing is, I have lots of gear that will have to come with us. Government-issued type of stuff, if you know what I mean. I already raided the station in town here. They had enough in the station to outfit a militia. Riot gear and everything. The fuzz. Because they had to be ready, if the government ever gave the word, to bring their boot down on the people.

This whole thing, you watch. This whole thing was years in the making. There have been warning signs. About this. What's going on. The government just tried to cover it all up. Didn't want people to know the real story. But I know a lot of shit. Like, classified shit. The shit the government don't want anyone to know about.

We'll hit my bunker, gear up. Get you going to where you need to go. I'll get to stretch my legs. And I can tell you all about it. The whole story. What the fuck's been happening to all of us. The real history of the world. That's what I got. This is fate. You were sent to me.

You look too soft for all of this.

When I was your age, I was a fucking animal.

I'll take you under my wing.

But turn the recorder off, first. I gotta show you something.

3.

EM, 42 (???, ON)

EM: Yeah, so my name is Em Murrell, and I'm here right now with Lowell Garrish, and now we're on the road and still in one piece, right, Lowell? Hey! Wake up. If you don't fucking answer me when I ask you a question, I'll hit you with the baton again. On the other side of the head this time, so fucking talk when I tell you to.

LOWELL: Yes, sir.

EM: Don't call me sir. This isn't the fucking army. I've taken you under my wing. You call me Father from now on, okay? What do you call me from now on?

LOWELL: Father.

EM: That's right. Because I'm looking out for you, right?

LOWELL: Yes, Father.

EM: That's right. Now, we're gonna have to start at the start and work our way all the way to the end. Which is now, is what I'm saying. Aliens, Lowell. Aliens flew here from another galaxy, and they were looking for a planet with certain conditions that could sustain life, and they came here, they found Earth, and Earth was perfect. So they decided to start their clone farms here on Earth. But there were all these dinosaurs on the Earth, so they had to go around and kill them all off. They flooded the air with all of these fucking reptile viruses, and the viruses killed off the dinosaurs. Viruses that would kill reptiles but that mammals were immune to. Because the aliens, at their core, they're mammals, just like us, Lowell, that's what a lot of people don't know. You start talking about aliens to someone, Lowell, they start thinking about lizards or glowing light creatures or whatever, and maybe there are aliens out there in the universe like that, but the aliens that came to Earth, Lowell, they were mammals. And once all of the fucking dinosaurs were dead, that's when they started up all of their clone farms. And that's how primates came to be, Lowell. It's not like we evolved from fucking rats or anything, we were always primates. But all primates, they were created from these clone farms. And the cloning, the aliens, it was all trial and error for them, so some of the clone batches turned out differently than they were supposed to, and that's why you have different types of primates all around the world. Gorillas and Neanderthals and gibbons and howler monkeys and all of that. Different batches of clones turned out differently. But finally after a bunch of failed attempts the aliens managed to create batches of humans and that's how we came into existence. We were the end result of all of these failed experiments.

But what happened to the aliens, right? That's what you're wondering now, right? Why'd the aliens go through all of this trouble to clone humans and then just leave, right?

Well, here's the fucking kicker. Are you ready for this, Lowell? Only half of the fucking aliens left. The other half stayed here on Earth, and lived with the clones of themselves that they made. And they bred with them. And they assimilated themselves into the clone population. And this is how the aliens are trying to spread themselves throughout the universe. They come to a habitable planet, start up a clone farm, start up their new societies, and then move on to the next habitable planet. See, these aliens, they're not trying to become, like kings, or anything like that. They're just trying to spread their DNA across the universe. They're just trying to spread life around. They don't try to conquer things. They try to spread. Like a virus, kind of. That's their goal. Do you get me?

LOWELL: Yes, Father.

EM: The ones who stay, for a little while, they have knowledge of technology, and they try and pass that on the best they can through these clone societies, but eventually the aliens die, and most of the knowledge they have dies with them. Some of it gets passed down, but not all of it can. And that's why you see evidence of all of this crazy technology in ancient civilization. Shit like Stonehenge and the pyramids. They had the knowledge of how to do all of that because the knowledge was passed down to an extent, but eventually all knowledge gets lost as societies come to ruin, and wars destroy culture and so on and so forth, you understand?

We've got alien blood in our veins. The DNA doesn't fade. That carries on. That information survives; we can pass it on through our bodies. But information about technology and science that stuff can't be carried on like that. So it dies out. Gets covered by sand and silenced, et cetera.

Until eventually you have a society built up that has no idea how it got there. No idea how it knows anything at all. Like, a society of amnesiacs. And the governments, they know this. And that's where the hustle comes into play. Because there's no one easier to hustle that an amnesiac. You can tell an amnesiac anything, and they'll believe you because they have to. Because they got nothing else. They got a hole in their head where the truth used to be.

You can get an amnesiac to do anything you want to. You just gotta know to manipulate them. The governments, they know that everyone's missing something. And because they know this, they know they can manipulate us.

And the aliens that started it all off . . . they're light years away, spreading themselves around the galaxy. They got no interest in us as a kingdom. They got interest in us only as a mould. Or a fungus. Are you listening to me?

LOWELL: Yes, Father.

EM: Because this shit tires me out. I think about this shit all the time, and it tires me out. It's a burden, this knowledge. That's why you were sent to me. I can't carry all of this shit forever.

LOWELL: Yes, Father.

EM: Yeah, okay, that's enough for now. I'm fucking hungry. Turn it off.

4.

EM, 42 (???, ON)

I don't want you talking anymore during the recordings, even if I ask you questions, I don't want you to respond. I don't like your voice on them. The message, your voice is muddling the message of what I'm trying to talk about here, the information I'm trying to pass on to people so that's why I had to wrap the duct tape around your mouth today. Your voice it just messes up the message that I'm trying to send to people so it's just for safety's sake.

I had to hit the little dipshit again today because he dropped the bag he was carrying the tape recorder in. I don't know how any of it has managed to survive this long. How he carried it all the way here from Halifax is beyond me. How many times did you drop the tape recorder between here and Halifax, you dipshit?

This is going to be a miracle if any of this survives.

And I can't do anything about your eye, either, dipshit so you better stop your fucking whimpering. It's like having some kind of fucking dog or something. What do you call them? Chihuahuas? That whine at the door when they want outside or whatever.

Like at the prison back in Kingston. We didn't know what to do with the ones left in the lockup. The prisoners. A couple of my co-workers were looking after them for a while, sliding them meals and everything. Then when the town really started going south, a couple of them started suggesting we let them out of their fucking cells. Well, no fucking way to that, I said. That's when I had to start Operation Shutdown. Ralph, I had to shoot him. Burt and Adrian they got away. Managed to club Lester unconscious with the baton. Strung him up in the hallway, so all the criminals they could hear him screaming while I started skinning him there. Because I wanted them all to shut up. They'd all been whimpering. Like dogs wanting to go outside. For days. I knew that if I skinned Lester, they'd shut up after that. They did, too.

Locked and barred all the doors of the place and left them to finish serving their time.

They're still in there. And if they're not, whatever it is that's taking people now would have got them by now. The purple light horseshit.

I don't know where Burt and Adrian ran off to. Probably Toronto. But that was a month ago.

And to be honest, if Gananoque had some kind of military out-post still operating out of it, and Burt and Adrian made it there, why didn't they send anyone to Kingston? To help the prisoners. Or to hunt me down. That's how far the shit has flown. I'd be surprised if you even find anyone in Gananoque, Lowell.

You know, I passed Gananoque on my way to Brockville. I didn't see no military bullshit.

Which brings me to these fucking two letters you've been carry-ing, Lowell. The ones you're supposed to be delivering to Gananoque for the fuzz. From Lancaster. Have you read them? I know you probably haven't because the envelopes were sealed, but . . . I mean, I'm looking at both of them right now, and you know what? The letters are blank, Lowell. The paper . . . there's nothing on it. In the letters. It's just folded up sheets of blank paper. You don't believe me? Look. Here. Blank. Sheets. No words. Nothing.

Why'd they send you to Gananoque carrying blank sheets of paper?

What the fuck kind of sense does that make?

That make sense to you?

Fuckin' odd, isn't it?

They sent you out of Lancaster with a couple of blank sheets of paper.

There's a reason people don't trust cops, kid. There's a reason we call 'em pigs.

You can get a person with amnesia to do anything. They know this.

You're safe now. With me. I'll look after you. I'll show you the way, from here on out. I'll teach you the truth. And I won't ever lie to you. Have I ever lied to you? Lowell?

My father was a real card. He was a liar. He told my mother that he never did anything to us, growing up. He couldn't figure out why we were shitting the bed all the time. Even as teenagers. You imagine that? In junior high and still every once and a while waking up covered in your own shit? Having to throw out the sheets and scrubbing yourself before some rash set in. Before anyone else in the house woke up. And then getting fucking yelled at because where the fuck have the sheets from your bed disappeared to? Because we can't afford new goddamned sheets every week so where did they go, Em? And my father with that look on his face every time it happened. That look of feigned fucking bewilderment. "I don't know what's going on with them. I don't know why they're acting like this." The look on his face was so fake and stupid that it just made you wanna drive hot fucking stove irons through it.

We were under his wing until she died. Mom. And after she died, we clipped his wings with a sledge axe. In secret. In the garage. And we threw the pieces in the trash just like we had with our shit-stained sheets. And no one ever knew. No one ever found out. And after my brother hung himself in his twenties, I was the only one left who knew anything about anything. I was the only one anywhere, the only one at all who knew anything about anything. I was the only one left carrying around the truth.

If you ever bring this up again, I will break your skull. I'll rip that duct tape off and take my pliers and crack your jaw in half. I don't like talking about this shit. You make me talk about this again, and I'll break you into pieces so small they'll fit into a fanny pack. TURN THAT FUCKING THING OFF!

5.

EM, 42 (???, ON)

I've been listening to all of your old recordings, and I'm starting to think I've made a terrible mistake. I've been listening to all of the tapes and they're just . . . they're just really amateur, and I'm not sure if you're up to the task, to be quite honest. And understand that's me being honest. That's my honest opinion because I've never lied to you. Everything just sounds so amateur, like the things you've been recording, just random people talking out of their asses, and you never ask them questions and just the whole . . . lot of it. Just a bunch of nonsense.

And now with the state your leg's in after you made me kick you today. I don't know what you were thinking when you dropped the fucking rifle bag. Those rifles are fucking loaded. It's dangerous. What you did. Someone could have gotten hurt. I could have . . . you're a danger to yourself and the people around you, Lowell. I feel bad for Jane, having to put up with you as long as she did. And you couldn't even keep her safe. I mean, I'm starting to think I'm taking a real risk here, taking you anywhere.

And with your leg in the state it's in now, we'll be moving slower than fucking tree sloths like this. And what are we supposed to do now? What, you think I'm going to carry the fucking rifle bag now? Or the fucking recording equipment? You think I'm gonna carry the rations?

But the bigger problem, really, is just your whole . . . mentality, Lowell. Your just not as with it as I thought you were. You can't even see out of your left eye, anymore, can ya? Can ya? You can't. I bet you can't. Your other eye it looks glazed over. Like you got this glazed look on your face now. Like you're a fuckin' handicap or something.

And this is who I'm supposed to be sharing my message with? You're really gonna be the one who records my message? You're my prophet?

You weren't sent to me. I'm starting to understand that now. You weren't sent to me. I was sent to you. Put you out of your misery. You're just some brainwashed zombie kid the pigs in Lancaster were having some fun with. You're just another lost soul wandering around aimlessly, waiting for the purple light to come and collect ya.

And now you're putting me in this position. I'm in this position again, same position I found myself in two weeks ago with my last little buddy. Whatever his name was. The one I tried eating. But human flesh, Lowell, let me tell ya, human flesh is overrated. Like, I tried to, but I couldn't, not even with barbecue sauce and brown sugar. It didn't taste right. I just don't got it in me, I guess. I'm not savage enough to really . . . I couldn't make it taste good enough to stomach.

The sad thing is, is that it's the world, ultimately, that's going to suffer. The world, that's the real tragedy here. The world's never gonna hear my story. I'll never be able to share my truth with . . .

Unless I carry on your work for you. Take what you're doing and make it my own. Bear your cross.

I could take the equipment and start over. Start interviewing everyone I meet and get the real story out of them. Get them to tell me the real truth, behind everything. What they really think. What they really feel. I could do that.

I know how to ask questions. Being a prison guard, I had to ask people questions all the time. I had to interrogate criminals every day. Get them to spill their guts. Cut through all the bullshit. I was actually pretty good at that part. Cutting through the bullshit. Getting people to fess up. Getting them to rat each other out. That part of the job was easy.

I recognize you, Lowell. The work you were doing. I recognize it, now.

I see how it is important.

I don't think you're up to the task anymore, though. Not with your leg like it is. I don't think you can even see out of that eye.

There's no reason why I couldn't just pick up your work where you left off, you know? Where you leave off. No reason at all.

I could do this. Get my own message out. Carry my own words. Find out what's really happening to all of us while I'm doing it.

There's no reason why it can't be me.

I can absorb this.

I can absorb you.

It should be me.

From now on, it will—

End of tape #F-423B2.

6.

CASEY, 34 (GANANOQUE, ON)

CASEY: Believe it or not, that was the first person I've ever shot. Being a medic, I haven't really run into an instance where I've ever really had to pull a trigger. I've had to draw my gun a few times, but never, well . . . never had to shoot anyone before.

Wasn't as hard as I thought it would be, though. Didn't mean to hit him in the head like that, but, oh, well! He was sticking you with his knife, right? I mean, can't be going around sticking people with knives like that. Someone might shoot you, if you do. Am I right? Ha!

So we've stopped the bleeding, and bandaged up your leg. You're lucky that he only kind of scratched it with his knife. We've disinfected and cleaned up your eye, and that patch should be all the protection you need until it heals. I think he might have detached your retina, which would explain the loss of vision on that side. But it'll heal itself up. Just keep the patch on.

Your knee is going to give you some problems. It's bruised pretty badly, and I think he might have knocked a chip off your tibia or your kneecap. That would account for the swelling. But I don't think any of your ligaments are ripped. Maybe a little cartilage. The knee's going to be swelled up for a bit, and it's not going to go down until you rest it for a while.

It looks like you may have suffered a couple of concussions. Which I can't really do too much about. Sorry. Wish I could, but I don't really have anything for that at the moment. Other than the Aspirin. Again, with the concussions, just like the knee injury, the only thing you can do is rest. Takes time in both cases.

You should come into town with me. There's no outpost or anything, I'm not sure where you got that idea. There's a bunch of us set up in a bed and breakfast on the west side of the community. I'm the only military personnel. I got separated from my squad a few weeks ago when we were patrolling outside of Kingston.

The bed and breakfast is all right. We got a couple of gas generators set up there, and so we have lights and stuff in the house at night.

There are groups of people, kind of sporadically spread around here and there. If you don't want to chill with us you should be able to find someone. The world isn't completely empty yet.

Don't ask me anything about what's going on, though. Because your guess is as good as mine. I only ever took orders. No one ever told me anything. I was just along for the ride.

I'd recommend you coming in with me, though. Stay with us until you're rested up.

This is going to sound really weird, but you look like my little brother. I haven't seen him since I got called to duty. He lives in Winnipeg. He's taller than you, but he has your hair. I am still hoping he's okay in Winnipeg.

So how long are you going to record me for?

LOWELL: As long as you keep talking.

CASEY: Oh. Okay.

LOWELL: It's nice.

CASEY: Nice?

LOWELL: Just hearing somebody talk that's not . . . that's not completely insane.

CASEY: Oh.

LOWELL: Thank you.

CASEY: Well. You're welcome. You are certainly welcome. What was your name again?

LOWELL: Lowell.

CASEY: That's a pretty name.

No, my brother, I mean. Growing up I was pretty protective of him. I think maybe that's why I keep thinking of him so much. Like, more than my mom or dad, or anyone else. I mean, I'm still worried about my mom and dad, too, it's just . . . I don't know. I used to look after my brother growing up. I don't know why that makes me think of him more.

Oh, there's something odd, too . . . if you're recording stuff. I know this is going to be weird . . . I got no one else to report it to, so . . . yeah, maybe it should be on some kind of record or something. Is that okay? It's just something . . . someone should record this.

I've stopped menstruating. I haven't had my period in two months. I haven't . . . uh . . . I don't know of anyone else who has, either. I've been speaking to women, like . . . looking after some women . . . and it's the same with all of us. I don't know if it's just isolated to this area or what, but . . . uh . . . no one's menstruating anymore. I don't know what that means. If our bodies are shutting down or what. Or if it's some kind of subconscious cultural thing or what.

But it's weird. Not normal. So there. Got that off my chest. Uh.

Let's get you to the bed and breakfast. You can sleep in my room. But only if we can spoon.

I'm just kidding. I'm kind of hilarious.

Here, let me help you up.

APRIL

LOWELL (GANANOQUE, ON)

I get these headaches now because of my eye. Trying to use my eye, I think, is what causes the headaches. Or maybe I'm still recovering from the concussions. It could be either or, really. I've been trying to rest here at the bed and breakfast in Gananoque.

Casey's . . . uh . . . their medic . . . she's been giving me lots of attention. I guess the people left around here see me as the closest to her in terms of age, so I guess, uh . . . that's why.

Because I've been resting for a while I've had some time to go over some of the interviews, label the tapes better and organize everything. Reread all the stuff in my notebooks about the wolves. The old stories I was writing. It's hard reading stuff that you've written so long ago. It feels like someone else wrote it.

Did you know that this is cottage country? Gananoque . . . it's scenic, really scenic. Part of the Thousand Islands. Because there's apparently more than a thousand of them. Islands. In the St. Lawrence around here. The glaciers formed them. Casey gave me some pamphlets. Very comprehensive pamphlets. These islands have been just sitting here for thousands of years. Ever since the glaciers tore them up. Leaving these islands all scattered out in the St. Lawrence.

Scattered, but they're still here.

I mean, the place is kind of touristy, but Jane would have liked this bed and breakfast. She would have liked the old-fashioned stove in the kitchen.

I should sign the guestbook before I leave, I guess, if they have a guestbook here. They should have a guestbook here. It's a bed and breakfast.

Or maybe that's not the most important thing.

I need to keep myself distracted, again. I could start working on the wolf stories again.

Except I'm a whole different person now.

I should leave soon.

1.

LES, 54 (GANANOQUE, ON)

We've been working together here for a while now. There are other spots in town like this. People living together. Working together. Now, with the snow gone, it makes things easier. We can just pop down the street real easy when we want to check up on each other. The winter was tough on everyone. The snow and everything. And then you'd eventually get around to checking on your neighbour or the old guy down the street, and they'd have gone missing in the night, that sort of thing. Casey's been a real godsend, because Bernice has got asthma and been having trouble breathing, as of late. Because she'll get claustrophobia and panicked, and we've been having to raid people's houses for extra puffers and the like. Scary business. But now Bernice can go outside, and we have Casey check-ing in with her so Bernice's going to be fine.

I think we're going to try and make a go of it here for as long as we can. We had a group come through the other day, said they'd come from Toronto and told us that Toronto was a real shitshow. They said they were heading toward Montreal to see if things were any better there. But I guess they aren't, are they? Too bad you weren't here to tell them that when they came through.

So I guess if I were you, and if you really are that gung-ho and determined to keep travelling, then maybe you should try heading over to the States. You could see if things are any better over there. I doubt it, but that's really the only other . . . option, I guess. If you follow the parkway east, you'll come to the Thousand Islands Bridge. You can cross over to the States there. I have no idea what awaits you, that way, but you could head over there, see what's going on.

Maybe the States are better off than us, but I doubt it. Haven't seen the lights on over there since February so I have no idea. There haven't been any planes flying overhead coming from that direction or anything. Come to think of it, I haven't seen a plane fly overhead since February or so, either.

We have seen the lights, on occasion. No one really wants to talk about them, but we've seen those from time to time. Hovering over the water. Whatever they are. All purple and everything.

UFOs, I imagine. Eh? What else could they be? Really. No one really wants to talk about them, but what else could they be, really?

They're sure as spitfire not the aurora borealis, that's for damn sure.

They're sure as spitfire not human.

It's like somethin' out of an Ed Wood movie, you know? I mean, with Ed Wood, it wasn't ever just aliens, you know? It could never be something as simple as that with him. It had to be aliens and vampires and giant squids all rolled into one. Which is why I always thought his movies were creepier than your standard science fiction fare. I mean, his movies, sure they looked more low-budget than most of the other movies of his day. But the ideas in them . . . the things that man came up with, the stories . . . he found some way of rolling them all together and making them creepier than your run-of-the-mill alien stuff. There weren't just aliens, but vampire aliens, a mix of the science fiction stuff with the occult stuff, and I think that was probably the thing he did best. His movies were shitty, but the ideas behind them could make your skin crawl.

And I wish it weren't like this, but that's what this all feels like. Like we're stuck in an Ed Wood movie. That's exactly what it feels like. Like maybe some alien's gonna abduct me tonight, or maybe it won't be some kind of alien, maybe it'll be some kind of vampire, instead. Or some kind of vampire alien. Or some kind of cosmic squid.

They're not your regular run-of-the-mill aliens. You wait and see. It's gonna be something weird.

I wish we were being invaded by some kind of . . . army, or something, you know? Because then whatever was gonna happen, it'd be over with by now. And people, all of us . . . we wouldn't be stuck inside of the real life Ed Wood movie. I mean, this isn't hell. What's happening to us. We're not in hell. We're in an Ed Wood movie.

You watch, you're going to cross that bridge, and you'll probably come face to face with zombie orangutans. It's going to be something weird like that, probably. Or mutant fish that can hypnotize people. Psychic robot crabs, or deeply sadistic zebras. That's what we're dealing with here. And I don't even believe in any of those stupid things.

I think we're dealing with something so weird no one would even bother to make a movie out of it. I think we're dealing with something so wacky that Ed Wood probably wouldn't even put it in his movie.

And that guy would put anything in his movie.

I'm gonna get ripped apart by robot crabs, you just watch. Something as dumb as psychic robot crabs.

And I don't even eat seafood. I'm a "landetarian."

2.

FAY, 32 (SELTON, ON)

We're trying again for a kid. Not because we're dumbasses or anything, but because that's how much faith we got in everything. In society and all that. This whole thing will right itself, turn itself around, people, they're gonna make their way through it and all that, and hopefully if Randall can knock me up in the next week or so, well, nine months or so from now, the hospitals will be back up and running, you just wait and see. We got faith.

We got faith because we have to have faith. In the world. In everyone getting everything back on track. Because the alternative means . . . well, I mean the alternative means, what? No playoffs ever again? That's frickin' dumb.

We don't mind sitting them out for a year. That's fine. We're adults. We can be patient. Even though the frickin' Maple Leafs were on a frickin' tear this year, and this year was probably gonna be their year, but whatever. Whatever. We can wait until next season. When they get everything up and running again. I'll be watching the Leafs on the flat screen again and knocked up with our third kid. Everything will be running again just like normal.

And even though it's frickin' bull, what's happening right now, frickin' complete bullpucky because this was the Leafs's frickin' year, ask anybody who knows anything about hockey, the frickin' bookies were even projectin' them as winners, such frickin' bullpucky that this is the year the frickin' world decides to slime its underpants.

Randall used to play before his knee got twisted to crap and he pulled his ACL, the ligaments, and that was it for him. And our two sons we had them enrolled, they were playing for Gananoque, the community there, and when we showed up to the area that morning back in January to pick them up and they just weren't there, well . . .

It's frickin' bull about the Leafs, the playoffs being cancelled. Because it was shaping up to be a beautiful season. It was shaping up to be our season. Me and Randall and Leo and Neil's. Leo was the older one, we told him to keep an eye out for his younger brother. And I'd like to think that, when I think about it, how they may have gone, or got taken or whatever, that Leo was near him. Near my baby boy, Neil. Looking out for him. That my boy, Leo, was protectin' my baby boy, Neil. Leo was such a good defenceman. And it's such frickin' bull because it was really shaping up to be our season and everything.

We're doing all the methods and positions and everything, me and Randall, I'm putting him through the paces about it, that's how much faith I got in the world righting itself. You watch, I'll be pregnant, and nine months from now, everything will be back to normal. We'll have another son, and we'll call him Patrick, and we'll be parents again, real actual parents again, and the Leafs, they'll still be in good shape. They're resilient. Something like this won't stop their momentum, you just watch. And they'll start winning, and it'll be a historic season for the Leafs, a championship season for the Leafs and for us, for me and my man, Randall, and our new son Patrick, just you watch. And Patrick, we'll name him Patrick Leo Neil Emerson. Because we won't forget either, we'll honour their memory, but everything will be back on track, too, and the Leafs will take an early leave, and it's going to be something to see, all right. So we can be adults. We can be patient for now, and put the loss of the season behind us. Because it's all ground we can gain again next year.

And like I said, I'm really putting Randall through the paces. All the positions, everything. The inside of that camper looks like a frickin' hurricane hit it. Hurricane of all of our fucking or lovemaking or whatever you want to call it. Harbinging. And then Patrick will be on the way just you wait, nine months from now.

It's frickin' bullpucky, but we're adults, and we can be patient about it. Get over the hump and have another baby boy, a hockey player, another little hockey player, like Neil or Leo, and everything will be back to normal and it'll feel like . . . it'll feel just like we never lost anything. Like we never lost the season, like we never lost my baby boy, like we never lost my period and . . .

I'm gonna be pregnant soon, you should see the positions I'm putting Randall through. We just gotta hang on and be patient, and the next thing you know . . . everything will be like it was, and all of this crazy bullshit will just be a dream. Just some kind of crazy bad dream, and we will have awoken from it and that will be that.

Hockey is like, in our blood. Randall is a good man. Hockey players are good men. They're like warriors. They don't give up.

He's been very good about all of the positions I'm putting him through.

We'll get our season back.

Us moving to this campground, this is just a temporary thing. We're doing what you might call regrouping, right now. Families do this all of the time. Regroup.

Trick to regrouping is patience. Patience and faith. And knowing who you are.

I might be pregnant already.

3.

WESLEY, 34
(THOUSAND ISLANDS BRIDGE, ON/USA)

WESLEY: Bruce and I . . . here in the station, it can get pretty boring at times. There haven't been so many people trying to cross as of late, so there's lots of time leftover to try and fill. We finished the crossword puzzles we brought with us a long time ago. We finished most of the books. I haven't finished Fyodor Dostoevsky's *The Brothers Karamazov* yet, but to be honest I've been having a hard time getting through it. He's real political and, to be honest . . . political seems so pointless nowadays.

It's been quiet here. There've been, what, Bruce? Maybe, like, five people we've seen in the past few weeks? We got enough time on our hands, is what I'm saying. We finished most of the books and crossword puzzles, so most of our reading now is repeat reading. Of the *Playboys* and *Hustlers*, mostly.

BRUCE: Miss March.

WESLEY: Yeah, no kidding. Miss March, she's this exotic lady who hasn't apparently shaved her bush, and Bruce and I apparently react to her the same way and everything. She's twenty-two years old and likes cycling and mountain climbing, and she's really not into guys who think that the world rotates around them, their egos . . . which kind of has been blowing our minds because Bruce and I are exactly the polar opposite of that. Those ego guys that turn her off. Miss March. Bruce and I, we get that the world doesn't revolve around us. If we were ever lucky enough to meet a girl with a bush like that

we'd be able to show her how we weren't like that. Those ego guys.
We'd be total gentlemen. Ain't that right, Bruce?

BRUCE: Yah.

WESLEY: First time I saw her I had to double-check the cover. Did
a double-check because I forgot if I was reading a *Playboy* because
she was showing her bush. And because she's exotic. Exotic and
showing her bush outside of *Hustler*? I mean, the world's moving
fast nowadays, but it's not moving that fast.

So she's out of bounds. She's off-limits for when we start up the
competitions.

Every once and a while, Bruce and I will start up a competition,
to help pass the time whenever we're real bored. Because we've
already finished the crosswords, and I'm not reading any more
Dostoevsky.

First guy to blow his wad wins. We count to three and then it's
every man for himself. And I got my technique down pretty good
at this point, old Bruce here, he can't match me. What are ya now,
Bruce? Forty-eight years old? My best time is three minutes, thirty-
four seconds.

But you let me look at Miss March while I'm doing it? One day I
actually did it in one minute, thirty-two seconds. No bullshit. That
girl makes me lose control, man. I can't even explain it. And to tell
you the truth, I'm not sure what it is about her that does it. You'd
think maybe it was her bush, her nice hairy bush bristling out of
that perfect skin of hers. Or the perfect size of her breasts . . . they
aren't big at all, but they're what you would call memorably unique.
Her legs are fantastic, but that's not, I don't think, what makes me
shoot my wad so quick. And it ain't something dumb and romantic-
sounding like her eyes, either. I mean she has nice eyes. Eyes that
make you think they got solar systems inside of them, but it ain't
her eyes that make me shoot off so quick. It ain't that.

So, what makes me lose my load?

It's the stuff about her in the information section that gets me
going. How her turn-offs are guys who have these egos that think the

whole world revolves around them. Because I'm not that guy. I don't ever want to be that guy. I'm the opposite of that guy. Which makes me perfect for her. And she's obviously not just some jerk lady, either. She mentions how she enjoys those Darren Aronofsky movies so she must be fairly . . . worldly, you know? And she has the bush . . . like, she could have shaved for the photo shoot but she didn't. And this is *Playboy* after all, so, yeah. Kind of a badass. Smart badass worldly girl. Two minutes or less. Because I am fucking amazing.

Ask Bruce. Fuckin' Bruce. The guy fuckin' snores. In his sleep. And twitches. Like a terrier. He's asleep now, isn't he? Bruce? Fell asleep on us.

The girl in the magazine, Miss March. I'll never meet her now. I know that.

I'm sitting here in this toll station, with the last other guy I worked with who was single and wanted to hole up here with me to wait this thing out . . . what's the difference? Me jerking off to this girl in a world that's ending around me, versus some life where I live without jacking off, never even knowing this girl existed in the first place.

If I die alone, either way. What does it matter if you jerk off competitively with your co-worker to pass the time? If I die alone, either way. What does it matter if we've completely stopped asking questions to people crossing the bridge? If both sides are fucked?

I came here from the States. And these booths, you see how they're set up? We can only see the States, through the windows of these booths. We can only look back the way we came. We sit in booths, looking back at the way we came here from.

I see a girl, in a magazine; it gets me off that I still have some kind of chance with her. Because she looks like where I came from. Even if she is exotic. And everything's set up in these magazines for us to see her like that. Everything's set up so that we're always looking back.

The record I set for coming is one minute, thirty-two seconds. And just between the two of us? I know I'll never be able to get back there again. I won't. But I keep looking back at it, you know? Keep looking back at the States.

4.

MARA, 64 (GANANOQUE, ON)

I'm fairly certain that we're the last people left in Gananoque.

We just woke up two mornings ago and everyone else was just gone. Harold had a hard time with that. He was in a bit of shock, until you got here.

The people in the library. Casey and her group over at the bed and breakfast.

We woke up Thursday morning, and we just couldn't find anyone.

And we didn't know where to go because we didn't know what had happened. Me and Harold had slept right through the night. We slept through everything.

We couldn't decide whether we should leave town, or whether or not we should hide in our basement.

So we didn't do either. We just kept going around as usual. Pretending like everyone else was away on some kind of big trip or excursion.

And then you showed up this morning.

After having left us two weeks ago.

And you've made Harold so happy. He's happier today than I've seen him in months. That's why he's gone off looking for some wine for us all to have for supper. Normally he just goes puttering off to the library or down to the wharf to look at the water.

He's happy because you showed up again this morning.

Lots of people have left us. That's why. Lots of people have left. In the night. When we weren't looking. When we were asleep. Harold and I . . . sometimes I think we can sleep through anything.

But no one's ever come back before. But you did. You came back.

Maybe the others will, too.

That's why Harold insisted. On the wine.

After you left, Casey kept talking about you. You made quite the impact on her.

I'm concerned. I'm concerned that every name I know in my head now is just a memory. Every name except mine, Harold's, and yours, Lowell.

Lowell. Still here with us.

5.

HAROLD, 64 (GANANOQUE, ON)

I think we're dealing with some kind of interdimensional being. Something that can phase out of this dimension and into the next. That's why no one's ever seen one of 'em. Anytime some human gets close to one, the thing just phases out of our dimension and into the next. That's why we never see them. They're around—we just don't see them. We can sense traces of them. But we never see the beasts ourselves.

I think something is hopping into our world, grabbing people, and then hopping back into their own dimension. Taking us with them.

Something that can jump through the binding laws of time and space.

That's what I think is happening.

Who knows why.

I don't know why. I don't know the "why" to all of this. Just the "how." Phase shifters. Dimension hoppers.

I can't talk to Mara about this because she just tells me to cool my jets.

Mara doesn't believe in anything she can't see.

Given the circumstances, that can be pretty frustrating for a fella like me who's just trying come up with an explanation for it all. Why the hell this world doesn't exist anymore.

I want to hope they're not cannibals. I hope they're not . . . people eaters. Holy shit. People eaters. I just remembered that. My dad always used to try and get me going when I was a kid. He'd start singing some song about purple people eaters. Ha. Long-legged purple people eaters. Ha. Long enough to step outta one world and into another.

Jesus, I hope they don't eat people. Because there have been a lot of real nice people who're gone now. I don't want to think of them as some people-eater's lunch.

So that Casey girl was your sister? Or your friend?

The sunset through the trees is quite nice, right now. The quiet is nice, too.

We should get back to Mara. I'll carry your recording stuff, if you grab the two cases of wine.

Hopefully, those dimension hoppers leave us alone for the evening. Or at least, I hope they leave us alone long enough to get drunk.

6.

HAROLD/MARA (GANANOQUE, ON)

MARA: When I first saw him, I thought he was all right.

HAROLD: She had this look of terror on her face.

MARA: No.

HAROLD: At the junior high dance. This was back in the old days before lawsuits so the teachers had spread sawdust all across the floor of the gymnasium, so the floor was quite slippery.

MARA: Yes, I forgot about that.

HAROLD: And most of the night me and my buddies, Tom and Ike and Hester we were just running around like fools, and sliding around in our sock feet.

MARA: You took your shoes off at the door. Everyone took their shoes off.

HAROLD: And we were sliding around all over the place, just having a time.

MARA: And me and the girls, Harriet and Velma and Kate, we were all sitting along the side just watching everyone and talking about how everyone was dressed.

HAROLD: Watching us, our lot, me and my friends running around and making fools of ourselves.

MARA: I didn't even notice him. I didn't really know who he was. But Harriet, Velma, and Kate and I were too busy talking about everyone's dresses and—

HAROLD: And I'm slipping and sliding around like some kind of maniac on the sawdust on the gymnasium floor.

MARA: Just another boy. Dressed up by his mother.

HAROLD: They would play these slow songs, every now and again, in between the rounds of fast songs . . . every twenty minutes or so there'd be these slow songs—

MARA: We had our favourites, of course.

HAROLD: But so, during these slow songs, the teachers would get right angry at us if we kept sliding and running around. So we didn't have any choice. We had to quit horsing around when the slow songs came on.

MARA: And Harriet and Velma, they'd always have all the boys coming up to them, wanting to dance with them.

HAROLD: So we'd have to sit and wait during the slow songs. Me and Tom and Ike and Hester.

MARA: They were a crew. We didn't pay any attention to them.

HAROLD: But it was so slow during the slow songs. We were just kids. Could not figure out what to do with ourselves, for the most part.

MARA: We were watching Harriet and Velma, dancing away with their beaus. Because they really did have the pick of the litter. Velma was very pretty. Harriet, she was skinny as a rake.

HAROLD: So your gaze would inevitably wander.

MARA: Commenting on dresses and the whole while trying to figure out what made Harriet and Velma so special that they had all of this activity going on around them.

HAROLD: I mean, out of the sheer agony of boredom, your gaze would wander.

MARA: It was probably their dresses. That caught people's eye, you know. Because we knew Harriet and Velma. And we loved them; they were our best friends, those girls. But there was nothing special about them. In their brains or anything. Velma was never going to leave town. Harriet was pretty bad at French immersion.

HAROLD: And I don't know if she was aware of how she was looking at me or not.

MARA: I was looking at everyone; I was trying to figure out what made some people so special.

HAROLD: And our eyes met.

MARA: I realized I was looking at one of the boys that had been running around.

HAROLD: I had come to the dance dedicated to raising hell and acting out. But when I saw her . . . when my eyes caught her eyes—

MARA: And I could only think, "Oh, shit"—

HAROLD: Something inside of me that I didn't even know was there, it shot me out of my seat and across the gymnasium floor straight at her. Directly at Mara in her dress, which was red with white bows—

MARA: My mother had been sewing it for months. She put so much time into this dress for me for this dance—

HAROLD: And you find yourself in one of those waking time moments. One of those moments where everything is heightened but you kind of feel like fate or something is intervening and you can't control yourself—

MARA: I didn't really hear him, when he asked me, at first.

HAROLD: She had to get me to repeat it.

MARA: The "will you dance with me," and with these eyes.

HAROLD: And the moment of terror. Because she was fixated on me, I could tell, but I'd never done this before and—

MARA: He held out his hand. Like a complete little gentleman. And you try saying "no" to that.

HAROLD: She took my hand. And it was the first time. A girl holding my hand. With any kind of intention behind it.

MARA: It was very nice of him to ask.

HAROLD: And we danced.

MARA: And we danced.

HAROLD: I didn't try to kiss her or anything.

MARA: He was a complete gentleman.

HAROLD: But I could feel her. Everything about her was electric. Every time her hip brushed mine or our chests touched.

MARA: I tried hard to keep the distancing appropriate.

HAROLD: Back then, for a slow dance, you'd be an appropriate distance apart.

MARA: But the feelings were still there.

HAROLD: You didn't need all of that bumping and grinding you see nowadays on TV. People . . . just regular life and courtesy were enough back then. We didn't need the crutch of sensationalism that kids today seem to need to know what the fuck is happening.

MARA: He smelled like leather.

HAROLD: She smelled like vanilla.

MARA: I don't know how long the song was that we danced to.

HAROLD: Under five minutes for sure.

MARA: But we were an item after that.

HAROLD: I forgot about whatever me and Tom and Ike and Hester had planned.

MARA: We kept looking at each other for the rest of the evening. I couldn't take my eyes off of him.

HAROLD: She was the prettiest girl I'd ever seen. And I had seen her before at school. But after we danced, she was . . . after we danced, that's when I knew she was the prettiest girl I'd ever—

MARA: And after the dance, he would come to visit me—

HAROLD: At her house. Her father was never super keen about it.

MARA: And he proposed to me before graduation. And Harriet and Velma and Kate got so jealous.

HAROLD: I don't know how I knew. I just knew.

MARA: I didn't care. I just knew.

HAROLD: We just knew.

MARA: We just knew.

HAROLD: As much as she drives me crazy now.

MARA: He's clumsy. You can't take him into a store. He's too clumsy. He breaks things.

HAROLD: She thinks I should be able to read her mind or something.

MARA: He will stand in the middle of a room, thinking about something. And you can't move him. You have to hit him to snap him out of it, just so you can get by him.

HAROLD: I keep forgetting to lock the door at night.

MARA: He doesn't ever lock the doors. Even now. I keep telling him, but he keeps forgetting.

HAROLD: She keeps reminding me, but—

MARA: He cannot keep it in his head. Not at all.

HAROLD: I'm working on it, though.

MARA: He used to be a lot worse.

HAROLD: I did. I was. Worse. She's keeping me on the ball.

MARA: He's good so long as you stay on him.

HAROLD: She's the only reason I'm still here, probably.

MARA: He's just so clumsy.

HAROLD: This wine has quite the kick to it, eh, Mara?

MARA: It's good.

HAROLD: Lowell looks like he's almost dozing off.

MARA: Well, let him rest, Harold. He's been on the road for days.

HAROLD: I am certain the world could end and we'd be just the same.

MARA: There's no changing him.

HAROLD: These dimension hoppers . . . Bigfoots, whatever . . . they find us, they can't change us.

MARA: We'll always be the same.

HAROLD: We'll always be those kids on the dance floor.

MARA: That's what I tell him. That I always keep seeing him like the boy who—

HAROLD: I keep remembering her like that. When our eyes first met.

MARA: Like we've carried the moment with us. Through all of this. The moment we fell in love.

HAROLD: Bigfoots or whatever . . . we'll never change.

MARA: We'll always be us.

HAROLD: We'll always be us.

MARA: Dance partners.

HAROLD: Dance partners. I'm going to open another bottle of wine.

MARA: I don't know, Harold. You've drank a lot already.

HAROLD: Not for us. Look at him.

LOWELL: Me? Oh, no, I'm—

HAROLD: You're worried about Casey?

LOWELL: No, I'm—

MARA: She was a very nice woman.

LOWELL: Jane.

HAROLD: Eh?

LOWELL: Jane.

HAROLD: Jane? Who's Jane?

MARA: Pour him another glass, Harold.

HAROLD: Okay, hon.

MARA: You just need to rest. You're overtired. All of the walking you've been doing on that leg. You need to rest.

HAROLD: Take a break, kiddo. Have another drink.

7.

ANGUS, 33 (HIGHWAY 401, ON)

It's not like I ain't used to losing shit. Or being given shit and then having it taken away.

I appreciate you walking with me. For a ways, anyway.

I used to work at a factory. Was workin' there for ten years. Really liked the place. But one day we got this new manager, and me and him didn't get along, so the next thing I knew, my name started getting brought up on the short end of his monthly reports to the boss. Then, for a while there, the job turned into a type of hell. Until I got fired. I wasn't surprised that I got fired. I knew the instant my boss had taken sides with that new manager the first time . . . From that moment on, I knew my time in the place was limited. And I had been there ten years. Worked my ass off for that company for ten years.

Ten years, though, is nothing, when it comes to industry. Or business. Guys involved with business, they know that. They set that marker amongst themselves a long time ago.

Some excuse was generated. They found some new numbers to track, and all of a sudden, some quota wasn't being met, conveniently, for this new manager who didn't like me. So I met my end that way. It was unceremonious. I didn't even empty my locker.

I didn't care about the contents of the thing. Like I said, it's not like I ain't used to losing shit.

And so I moved on to some shittier job. Moved into a smaller apartment. Girlfriend left me because down wasn't one of the directions on her life compass.

I kind of liked that next job. Made a few friends. But the turn-over rate was high. It was a hotel, where I was working. They'd fire people for not wearing black socks, sometimes.

I was let go from there too, eventually. Same reason. Some guy in management found some new numbers to track, and I was not in line with the new quota.

Moved onto a much shittier job. A bottle-recycling place. The people I worked with there didn't want to even make friends. The customers treated us with about as much respect as the dead mice stuck to the bottom of their bottles. I took on the odours of the place. Ended up smelling like beer even though I wasn't drinking. My hands would get so black from the glass and the shit smeared all over the bottles that I couldn't look at them, end of the day.

And then my till didn't add up one afternoon. So I got let go from that. Just some guy on the wrong side of the numbers who couldn't even get a reference letter from his previous employers.

It was around then that the world started falling apart.

The whole business did not catch me off-guard. I had been pre-pared for constant decline.

People prepared me for it. People had prepared me for a world with no people.

And I don't mean to say this coldly. Or all emo-like. Along the way, my journey, my jobs, I cared about everything. Everything I was doing, all the people I worked with. I cared.

But me caring has never ever translated into me keeping.

That's what I've learned.

That's what I know now.

Me caring has never translated into me keeping.

I walk this highway expectin' less and less each day. And, as such, occasionally, I am pleasantly surprised with what crosses my path.

I appreciate you walking a ways with me.

I don't expect you to stay by my side.

And if you do, I won't get attached to yer presence, either. Promise.

MAY

LOWELL (HIGHWAY 401, ON)

We had burrowed into the snow next to Sertan's frozen corpse and were relying on the shelter it provided to protect us from the wind and snow. As Xyla huddled next to me for warmth, both of us were silent. I spent the next eternity reliving my life over and over again inside my mind. The birth of Xyla and Cabo. The death of my mother. The attack of the Desperate Ones. Memory after memory. Until everything began to fall away from me.

Every moment of joy. Every instance of despair. Every tragedy. My family, my hopes and dreams, exploding with vibrant colours in my mind before fading to void. I knew we would die here. Xyla and I. The last of us.

And as Xyla's shivering stopped, I could not help but feel a deep pride and love for our pack. Despite the tragedy of our song, we had always tried. My final moments were filled not with despair, but with love.

1.

SYLVIA, 41 (HIGHWAY 401, ON)

It's probably been a week by now. Said he'd be right back. I didn't know what he was up to. I woke up feeling kind of drug out that morning, you know. Body didn't want to move that much. I was too tired, for whatever reason, to bother to question him about it. I was too tired to worry about him. I was just groggy, I guess.

But, after an hour passed, I was up and about, and that knot started tying itself in my stomach again. I tried to not think too much about it. I tried to absorb myself with organizing our gear, then cleaning the cottage, weeding the garden just outside of the door here. I remember pulling up a few weeds, and squeezing them hard in my fist. I remember the scent of the earth, how it was cold and squishy. I remember holding my breath at certain points and sitting back and just trying to listen to the forest. For anything. For any little sound. I needed to hear him coming home, trudging through the brush. Him maybe chopping a tree down somewhere with his axe, in the distance. He did take his axe with him, so at first I thought that might have been what he was up to. Chopping a tree down for us for some reason.

By about noon the knot in my stomach was pulling itself so tight, I could hardly stand. It was making me wheeze, and the whole cottage seemed like it was spinning.

I know I fainted, at some point. Time gets kind of funny when you're alone. I remember opening my eyes, and I was lying on the floor, staring up at the ceiling of the cottage. The colour of the rays of light coming through the window was pink, and I knew we were getting close to dusk.

Something made me get up.

Somehow I managed to pull myself to my feet, went outside, and I started a fire in our little makeshift firepit. Dad had decided we wouldn't have any more fires outside at night. We didn't know what was out there after all and Dad didn't want us dragging any more attention to ourselves than we absolutely had to.

But that night, I couldn't stop myself. I don't know if part of me thought he might be lost or what. If me starting a fire, if he saw the fire, that might be the beacon he needed to find his way back to me. Even if it made him angry. I didn't care. I didn't care if he came back pissed off. I just wanted him to come back.

So I let the fire grow and grow. Started with a teepee of kindling first and, eventually, built a little cottage around it using some of the bigger cut pieces that we had stockpiled a few weeks earlier. And the fire kept getting bigger and bigger, and I kept staring at it, putting more wood on it. But the whole time, listening.

And I don't know how far it was into night. But at some certain point, I just had this chill wash over me. My whole body. Bumps popping on the back of my neck, and I knew. I just knew. For certain. Something had happened. He was gone. He wasn't coming back.

And so I stopped listening to the woods. And all I could do was stare at the fire.

I remember camping with my dad years earlier. When I was a kid. With him and Mom and my brother, Stevan. Whenever the fire got to that point. Where we were letting it burn out. My dad, he'd always look at the embers of our campfire and he'd point them out to me. He'd say, "Look at those. You know what those are? Those are the lights in the city at night." And then we'd watch them. Watch them as they slowly disappeared into darkness. One by one. Lights fading out. And then the fire was gone.

When Mom left us, she took Stevan with her, because he was still young. And Dad, his drinking got worse. And he was using it as a crutch for things he was missing and . . . well, I mean, he got fired for swigging from that mickey when he was on shift.

When we went camping after that, me, I was a teenager by that point. We'd stare at the fire, watch the fire turn to embers. And watch the embers wink out. One by one. "There goes the city." He'd say. Almost like the city was leaving him. Like it was leaving him to be alone by himself.

Our last fire together. Two weeks ago. We were staring at the fire together. Watched the flame turn to embers. And the embers started fading. And I knew what he was thinking. I knew what he was going to say. Except he never said it. We just kept staring at the pit until it turned black.

When you came walking out of the trees this afternoon, I knew you weren't him. I knew you weren't Dad. Dad is gone. Has been for a week. But I wanted you to be him. I wanted you to be.

I'm sorry.

I don't have any food for you outside of a carrot or two.

And I'm going to need you to leave here in the morning.

But I'm not going to leave.

I know he's gone. But I'm not leaving till he comes back.

2.

ESAU, 71 (HIGHWAY 401, ON)

Forget the interview. Because we got deals for you, brother. We got deals for you! You can pick things up here! Things that have meaning! Things that resonate, brother. In your soul, brother. That's what I mean when I say we got deals, brother. This wheelbarrow isn't just a wheelbarrow. This wheelbarrow is a cradle for lives that have been lived.

I have, for you, this wallet. Taken from a very big man. Big, like Goliath. Tall. More than seven feet tall. In Kingston, I met him. And when they take him, they leave this behind. His wallet. You can see all of the details of his life from this. His driver's licence. He was fifty-five years old. You can tell the details of his life from this. This is not just a wallet. This is a story. And stories? Stories keep you warm, brother. They keep you warm when you are alone.

And then I have this. This is a hatchet, brother. Very sharp, good condition. But it is more important that this hatchet was the property of a young man, brother. This young man, he was my friend. He was very close to me. We travelled together for weeks. But when they took him, they left his hatchet. And now here it is. Do you want it? It is a good hatchet. Used to build many lean-tos. To split much firewood. See the sheath? He carried it on his belt, always. This young man. My temporary friend.

Here is a dress. I never met the woman who wore it. I found it hanging in the closet of a house I stayed in one night. The house had no people in it. They must have been taken a long time before. And I found this dress in the upstairs closet. Here, feel this dress. Touch the dress with your fingers. Feel the materials on your fingers.

Now, imagine the dress on a woman. She was very beautiful, this woman. She was in some pictures I found in the house. Her hair, it was blond. She had a husband and two children. I think they were her children. I never met them. I never met her family. But I saw them in the pictures I found. I stayed in this woman's house for a night last month. During a bad storm. This woman was very nice to me. I never met this woman. But I would have died if I had been outside in the storm. This woman was very nice to me. I never met this woman. But she let me stay in her house. Feel the material with your fingers. It is very soft. I think she must have been very kind.

There are many things I have here. In my wheelbarrow. I carry them with me because I am not sure why. Sometimes I do not know why I pick them up. Sometimes, I know they hold stories, but I do not know what stories they hold.

This is a plastic bird. A flamingo. It is pink. I took it from someone's front yard. I do not know why I took it. I was walking through a town a few weeks ago. I saw this plastic bird. I could not stop looking at it. No one was around. The street was quiet. I was alone. And I could not stop looking at this bird. It was all alone. The only decoration in someone's front yard. Like it was all alone. Like it was standing guard. I do not know why. But I took it. They are called flamingos.

They are made out of plastic.

Turn off the recorder. You do not have to record this. There is nothing to record. There is no one here. Just me. And even me, I am not here. I am not here. Just this wheelbarrow is here.

The big man is not here. Just his wallet. The lady she is not here. Just her dress is here. I am not here. I do not think I am here anymore. Just this wheelbarrow is here. That is all that is left of me. It is all that will be left when they come and take me.

Do you want it now? Do you want anything here? When you think of them, these things, like stories, then you want them. That is how I used to feel. And so I would pick things up and put them in my wheelbarrow. And I came to love these things I would find. Because I would think of them like stories.

But recently, I have stopped thinking of them as stories. Recently, I have started to think of these things like they are people. They are all that is left.

That is why I say that I am not here, right now, talking to you. All that is here is a wheelbarrow. Because that is all that is left of me. And it is filled with things that are all that is left of people.

And I have been collecting these things for more than two months, brother.

I think I must have been crazy when I started doing it. I am worried that part of me has gone crazy.

But whether I am crazy or not, I know this to be true: I am not here.

So don't bother recording me.

I am just this wheelbarrow.

That is what is happening to me.

3.

CALLIE, 37 (SHANNONVILLE, ON)

What I've ended up missing the most, through all of this, besides television . . . and with the loss of television, I mean, we all took a big hit on that one. I still don't fuckin' know who won the last season of *Survivor*, which I'm still kinda fuckin' pissed off about, I probably shouldn't get myself going about that one.

How stupid people are. Is the thing that I miss the most. Without people around so much anymore, that's what I miss. Without civilization happening around us . . . I miss how stupid people can be.

People mowing their lawns wearing nothing but flip-flops. I miss watching people do stuff like that. Families with small children keeping giant dogs as pets. People forgetting to leave the emergency brakes on in their vehicles and watching their cars roll backward down the hill, in the city. I miss watching people chugging beer out of funnels and getting into fights with each other because they're too drunk to understand what the other is saying. I miss people texting while they drive. I miss people locking their keys inside of their cars and then having to try and break back in through the driver's side windows with a coat hanger. I miss seeing people driving Hummers. I miss seeing lazy newspaper delivery guys just throwing the paper at the house. Not aiming. Not even trying to get the thing on the step. Just chucking the thing in the building's general direction.

I miss hearing people telling racist jokes. And sexist jokes. And complaining about how minorities or women are getting paid too much, or are stealing jobs away from young white men. I miss hearing people getting all pissed off about turbans. I miss hearing about politics. Every stupid political thing ever. Senators spending the government's money to cover their own personal vacations. Members of Parliament getting caught for tweeting things they shouldn't, or saying things they shouldn't. I miss hearing about celebrities getting caught cheating on their wives with their maids or nannies or gardeners or tennis instructors or whoever. I miss hearing about people making mistakes on live television. Not being able to pronounce some game show contestant's name or whatever.

I miss hearing about how stupid people are. That's what I miss the most.

I don't want to be the last person on Earth, ever. Because that'll mean that I'm the stupidest person on Earth, and I don't want that.

I want there to be people left, so I can make fun of them.

Because when you can make fun of people, you don't have to think about yourself so much. Everything that's wrong with you. Everything you've done wrong in your life.

The less people around you, the more you focus on yourself. The hell that is yourself.

4.

BIRD, 32 (TYENDINAGA, ON)

This is how life is. All of these episodes . . . you think you have run into a dead end. You think you have hit a wall of solid brick. But then . . . pop! All of a sudden you find yourself on the other side with no idea how you got there, and nothing but fields of fresh fuckin' wheat stretchin' out in front of ya, far as you can see. Endless fields of fresh fuckin' wheat. Like staring at the ocean if the ocean, instead of it being full of water, it was full of fresh fuckin' wheat.

And no one likes staring at a dead fuckin' end. Not ever. Dead ends are about the last fucking thing you wanta have to deal with. But they keep popping up, as you get older, and you and me, what'd you say your name was? Lowell? Lowell, I got it. Do you know what that word means in Mohawk? It means wise fuckin' warrior. Wise fuckin' warrior, that's what Lowell means. Eh? Naw, I'm just shitting ya, Lowell. In Mohawk, Lowell means "Really big cock." Eh? "Really big cock." I'm not shitting you, eh? Hey, would I lie to you? Would I lie to you? Do you think I would lie to you? I know you just met me and all, but . . . yeah, I was just making that up. It doesn't mean "really big cock." It means "wise fucking warrior." That's its real meaning, eh?

It's a good thing you showed up here too, Lowell. 'Cause I been looking for a wise fucking warrior to help me out. 'Cause I just realized this morning that I been staring at a brick fucking wall.

Janice Goodleaf, she was the last person left in town other than me. I been taking my bike out, ever since the snow melted, and I been cruising up and down the road this twenty-kilometre stretch. Just watching. Observing. Keeping track of the people we had left.

Janice, she was the last person left around here, though. And I'd take my little cruise on my bike every day at around noon and she'd always be lookin' at me. I'd always see her lookin' at me from the front window of her house.

So when I drove by yesterday and I could see that she wasn't at the window, I swung around. And parked my bike in her driveway and ran up her steps and started banging on the door and hollerin'. But I didn't hear anyone inside, so I had to bust the fuckin' door down. And there was no one inside. No one left in the place. Coals still fuckin' glowing in the fuckin' fireplace. But no Janice.

I walked around her house and her backyard lookin' for her, eh? And I started to kind of think that I wouldn't find her. And that made me angry. I don't know why, but that was my feeling at the time. So I just started trashing her house. I couldn't help it. Something about it just made me so angry. I started throwing chairs through her windows and overturning her table and breaking her dishes, and she had these little porcelain dolls . . . I stepped on all their fucking heads with my steel toes I was so angry. I destroyed her fucking house.

And when I had broken just about everything left there was to break I looked down at the floor and caught my reflection in all of these little shards of glass on the floor. And I don't think it was a mirror, maybe it was a mirror, but I think it was just like really reflective glass, and I could see all of these different pieces reflecting back at me. Like I was staring at myself except I was all in pieces.

So I left after that, because the place was freaking me out. She had a couple of Steamwhistles in her fridge, I took those with me, I don't know where she got those, but I drank them when I got back here to my place.

And I didn't really know what to do at that point, eh? I built a campfire in my backyard. Cooked some Zoodles in the can. Ate those. Drank some of Peter Canoe's moonshine, good old Peter Canoe, he gave it to me for Christmas five years ago. Looked at the stars. Smoked a joint.

Woke up this morning, came back outside, got the campfire going again. Just stared at the flames. I was staring at the flames, but it was like I was back in Janice's house again. Staring at the flames this morning just made me think of all the glass on her floor and how I was staring at it and just saw myself in pieces.

And I realized, you know? Now, in this place, I'm the only one left here. This place has become my dead end. I'm the last one. That's my wall that I'm hitting. So I got to break through it, somehow. I gotta find my way to the other side.

And then I saw you walking along the road, and I figured I should take that as a sign, eh?

I was just kidding about your name, eh? Lowell doesn't mean anything in Mohawk. That I know of, anyway.

But I think you should come with me. Because the direction you were walking, let me tell ya. There's nothing down that way. And if you're thinking of going to Toronto, you might as well forget about it. Because that place got fuckin' gang-raped, I guess. A couple of military fellas passed through here last week. They said Toronto's like a place where hope goes to die. I guess they were goin' AWOL or whatever.

So if Toronto's fucked, and if you say the States are fucked, and Montreal's fucked, then there's really only one place left to go, isn't there?

I got another motorcycle. I fix them up as a hobby. You could hop on my spare. It's a Kawasaki. It'll give ya sweet fuckin' ride, my little Kawasaki.

Drive north until we find ourselves on the other side of the fucking wall, you know?

First, though, we gotta do some mushrooms. And you're not allowed to say no.

Whether we get anywhere or not, we're goin' on a trip, us.

5.

YANA, 46 (BELLEVILLE, ON)

YANA: When we were younger, Anna and I, in Victoria . . . our families had immigrated there together. . . . My mother and Anna's mother were very good friends. So they were very happy when we became good friends, too. Anna and Yana. We were always spending time together. Always having fun together. Running around Victoria like two little squirrels. We joined the band together in school. After we quit the rowing team together, we were on the track-and-field team together. We would pass books between each other. I would finish reading a novel and then give it to her, and she would exchange that with me for one she had just finished. This is why I gave her my book when she met me at the train station in Toronto this past Christmas.

I never think of things in order. See what I mean?

But in Victoria, as children, and running. Track and field. She was always faster than me. I would always be trying to catch her. I could never catch her. We did the four hundred metres, and I only ever saw her back. Shoulders. Calves. Earlobes.

I'm still cold.

LOWELL: You're burning up.

YANA: And calm, too. When we were younger. Anna was always calm. Calculating. Precise. I was the emotional one. The fool. The impulsive.

I remember, once, we had to go on this field trip. Our science class in high school. They loaded us all up together on the

school buses and drove us north and out of the city to Goldstream
Provincial Park. To watch the salmon run.

Thousands and thousands of salmon are born there every year.
And then they swim out into the ocean until they mature. Then
they stop eating, and swim back out of the ocean and up the river
where they were born so that they can find another salmon to mate
with and then they just die.

Their bodies, exhausted, falling apart on them as they try and
muscle their way through it all. Upstream. All instinct. Skin peel-
ing. Scales flaking. Tails splitting. Colour fading. Falling apart. But
never stopping.

I didn't like it. The whole thought of it all. That these fish would
reach a point in their life where they were all instinct, and dying, and
mass struggling against a never ending current. This mass of a population fighting against current and all the while unstoppably eroding.

I remember Anna just looking at the river. Which was so full of
dying fish you couldn't see the bottom of the stream. "But that's
life," she said to me, "that's why it's beautiful."

I was so careless, growing up. I was the one who left first. Left
Anna alone on her family's doorstep as I hopped in Vasily's station
wagon heading east to Winnipeg. I was the one who tried not to
think about such things as . . . as . . .

Then you realize you have swam too far away from each other
and there is this desperate push to get back. That's why I took the
train from Winnipeg to Toronto this past December, leaving Vasily
to his own depression and devices. Anna had moved to Toronto to
be with her new husband, Jules. That's why I spent Christmas there.
Why we were together when the event started. And then . . . there
is no order, anymore.

As we ran into the core of downtown Toronto that night in
January, she was sprinting ahead of me, and I could not catch her.
And so many people were screaming around us, and I did not know
where we were. I only knew that we were somehow trying to get to
Jules. That Jules was downtown. That Anna was not calm anymore.
She was not calculating. She was running, sprinting. Falling apart.
Muscling through people and leaping barricades to get to Jules . . .

I remember passing a hot dog vendor with a sign on his cart that said, "End of the World Blowout." He was blasting polka music on his little stereo, and people were hanging around him, dancing and eating.

I remember running through a group of policemen. Anna knocked one over as she sprinted through. He screamed at us . . . I don't know what. My heart was hurting, my lungs, I could barely breathe, but I was so scared of losing her in all of it.

We ran past a university and turned onto Yonge and that is where we saw all of the tanks, military tanks, lined up and driving up the street. And people were screaming around us, and I could hear the whoosh in the distance, quiet but loud and I turned my head just enough to see the purple lights behind us, closing in. That's when the tanks started firing, and Anna ran into the lobby of an old building and I tried to follow her in but the building . . . the building, it . . .

It just exploded. And she was . . . I saw her run into it and it . . .

And then my body was flying. Thrown backward.

That's the last thing I can remember about it. Any of it. Toronto. Anna.

My best friend.

When I woke up, it was maybe a day later. Very bright light. Sun in my eyes, and I was in a stretcher, being carried by these military men.

They had established a temporary base on the outskirts of the city.

I spent the rest of January living inside the husks of several GO trains with any other civilians that they could round up.

But then they started disappearing, too. The military men.

And when there were too few left of them to try and keep us there any longer, me and a handful of others packed whatever we could scavenge together and began to head east. Because we thought it might be better out east. Maybe we could make it to the sea. Maybe we could find a boat. Leave the mainland. Maybe we would be safe in Newfoundland, or the Magdalene Islands.

Someplace where we would all stop disappearing.

Eroding. Flaking.

We travelled along the main highway for a while, in March, I think, until we lost someone. And then we lost someone else.

After that, we stuck to the smaller roads.

But it didn't matter.

By the time we reached the edge of this place, this town . . . Belleville . . . there were only three of us left. Myself, this young girl, who was originally from Iqaluit, and this shaggy man from Yellowknife.

Almost a week ago, now. In this town. It was just after breakfast. We were huddled together, looking at our map, and then we heard the whooshing sounds again. Nearby. Too close. So we all ran.

Scattered.

Into this place.

And I tried to turn my head as I was running to see if they were still with me. But they weren't.

So I tried to climb that construction scaffolding to see if I could see them from higher up.

And then my hand slipped and I fell.

And when I fell . . . when I landed and I heard the snap, I thought that was it for me. I thought that that was the end.

But then you and your friend showed up.

And you brought me here.

This restaurant.

And then you brought out your tape recorder.

And I thought that was something different.

That we might be something different.

But now, even your friend is gone.

But you've found the antibiotics.

And so that might be something.

It might be something.

But I'm still cold.

Yes, you're still here.

I'm still here.

But I can't help but think about Anna.

How she kept looking at the salmon, when we were young.

I didn't like the thought of it.

"But that's life. That's why it's beautiful."

6.

OLLIE, 64 (BANCROFT, ON)

He gave that mug to me as a gift. I can't remember when. Whether or not it was a Christmas present or a birthday present. But the whales on the side of it, they disappear when you fill it with hot water. Just wait until I get this water to boil and pour you your tea. The whales will disappear from the side of it. They come back after you drink your tea, though.

I am very lucky to have a wood stove. Justin decided that the cottage would be heated naturally, no oil furnace, that kind of thing. He'd be the one up at five in the morning starting the fire. We have the furnace down in the root cellar down below us. The vents carry the heat all throughout the house. Keeps the house very warm. I'm never cold. We were never cold.

I do all of my cooking now on the thing. I basically just boil vegetables from the cellar or cans of whatever I can find. I've started going into the stores, restaurants around here. When I can. Taking what I can for food to stock up. I cook everything right on the surface of the wood stove.

I have always been a terrible cook. You've been warned. I can make all right tea. But if you're staying for supper . . . and I hope you do stay for supper, it'd be lovely to have someone to talk to . . . don't expect any miracles. All I can do is boil things, or heat them up, and drown them in margarine and salt and maybe soya sauce if I got any of that left, but I think I used the last I had last night. Justin was the one who did all of the cooking here. I did all of the easy stuff. The no-brainer stuff. I'd do the dishes, and make the tea, and clean. I did a lot of the easy indoor stuff. He did the cooking and the outdoor stuff, like getting wood. We both kept the garden together, though. We'd take care of the garden together. We'd help each other with the garden.

Things are quiet enough around the lake here. We kind of always just did what we felt like. Life was slow-paced around here to begin with, is what I mean by that. So if Justin or I ever got on each other's nerves, one of us would just go for a walk. Or a swim in the lake. Or go fishing. Or read a book. I did most of the reading. Justin liked building furniture out in the garage. He had a pretty full setup out there. All of the equipment, you know, that he needed. He built this cottage himself, you know? Before I ever met him.

We met each other online. Oh, I miss the Internet! The Internet was so much fun! We met through a dating site, and he drove all the way into Toronto to meet me. I was a university professor at the time. History. Bored to tears with my job. We went out to this very nice restaurant downtown. And I could tell he was nervous. But I was nervous, too, so that was okay. And he couldn't stop talking about this place. His cottage. Because he knew everything about it, because he built it by hand, himself. I could tell he was really lonely, because, well . . . sometimes men will start these really big projects, you know?

Look at the detailing on that bannister. The amount of work he must have put into it. The cabinets in the kitchen! He made those. Not a crooked line, an off angle anywhere. Everything in this house is perfectly level. And he told me all about it.

When he drove me out here for the first time, I knew everything about the place already. He'd told me everything. How the wind sounds as it blows across the lake and makes the trees creak. How the patio winds around the north corner of the house and around to the west, so you can watch the sunsets over the water. The one spot in the parlour on the floor he screwed up on that squeaks every time you step on it. The pine walls and floors. I knew the place already. Felt like stepping into a good book.

So I stepped into it and I became a character and we began our story. We wrote many chapters.

But in November, Justin had to step out of the book we were writing.

At first, I kind of panicked, and I didn't know what to do. I locked all of the doors. I did an inventory of all of my stuff and everything in the root cellar. The only things close to a weapon we had in the place was the poker for the fireplace. I remember, I grabbed a hammer and some nails from Justin's tool shed and I started boarding up all of the windows inside of the house. And then the doors. And I was boarding up the last door, the front door, that one behind you there, and I was holding a piece of board across the door frame with one hand, and holding the board and holding the nail to the board so that I could hammer it in, because I had the hammer in my other hand . . . and I dropped the nail. It slipped out of my fingers. So I bent over to pick up this nail that I had dropped, and I threw out my back.

I threw out my back trying to nail my own front door shut. I could barely move for days.

So when my back got better. I decided to take all of the boards down again. I felt embarrassed for thinking that they might have done any good at all. I stopped locking the doors after that night, too. Because whatever it was had already gotten Justin. And if they or it or whatever wanted to take me, then all of my boards wouldn't be much of an obstacle.

The snow fell outside, I rarely had to leave. I went snowshoeing around the lake a few times in February. I read a lot. There were points where I missed Justin very much. I left the doors unlocked the rest of the winter. I've been surviving off of the squash and carrots and potatoes in the root cellar we took from last year's garden. There's still food left down there, I couldn't eat it all myself. In fact, now that I think of it, let me prepare you a bag full. There's plenty extra you can take with you. I don't mind sharing. Not at all.

You're going to be passing through Maynooth, if you keep going north. If you meet the gentleman who runs the general store up there, make sure you say hello. If he's still around, tell him Ollie Caverhill has opened up his cottage to the public, and he's more than welcome to stop by for a meal of boiled vegetables and a cup of tea. Tell everyone you meet, for that matter.

You seem like a good judge of character. Well-travelled.

JUNE (II)

1.

JULIA, 5 (MAYNOOTH, ON)

LOWELL: What's your name?

JULIA: Julia.

LOWELL: Julia? That's a pretty name.

JULIA: Thank you.

LOWELL: So, how old are you, Julia?

JULIA: Five.

LOWELL: Five. Wow. Where's your mom and dad, Julia?

JULIA: Gone.

LOWELL: They're gone. Okay. Where'd they go?

JULIA: The Bird People.

LOWELL: The Bird People? Who are the Bird People?

JULIA: They're just . . . they're just . . . the Bird People.

LOWELL: Okay, well—

JULIA: You should hide.

LOWELL: Okay, well—

JULIA: They're coming back.

LOWELL: Okay, but—

JULIA: Hide, stupid!

LOWELL: Wait. Hold on! Just . . . Julia! Come back!

2.

ZOE, 35 (ALGONQUIN PARK, ON)

I got stuck up here around the end of December. I'm single, and I didn't have anyone waiting for me back home, so I kind of just kept hanging around up here, patrolling and such. Welcome to Algonquin Park.

I've always liked this place, ever since I was a kid. Beautiful up here.

There are two other guests here in the park at this moment that I know about. There's some crazy old racist guy, insane fella. He's set up over at the Mew Lake Campground. Some guy named Mitch . . . I wouldn't advise getting too close to him. He's carrying a firearm, and he doesn't mind squeezing off a few rounds at you, if you get too close. He doesn't seem to be straying too far from the campground, though, so . . . so long as you stay away from his general vicinity, he shouldn't be too much of a problem.

The other one's a girl a bit younger than me, I'd say. Kind of a quiet lady. I think she's had a rough go of things, but who hasn't, eh? Said her name was Samantha. All done up in camouflage gear and everything. Loaded for bear. Huge backpack on her, bow and arrows, the whole works. Quiet, though. Speaking of which, I should hike up there, check in on her, see if she's still around or what.

Those things that have been taking everyone, don't worry they've been all through this place up here, too. The park ain't safe. I don't think nowhere's safe, but the park, it sure ain't safe, either. They been sneaking through here from the start. Snatching campers while they slept. My co-workers on patrol. Fucking things.

I have not seen one yet. But I did find a couple of tracks. Up around Burnt Island Lake last month. Down in this patch of mud near the shoreline. Only tracks I ever seen of them. Whoever they are.

That Samantha lady was headed up to Opeongo Lake, so I might take a trip up there today. Got nothing else to do, except drive to the other gates, check them out. I could give you a ride up to the access point, if you'd like. You can hang out, camp up there, or grab a canoe, go off wherever.

Just respect the other campers and don't start fires you can't put out. That's not just park rules, that's rules for life.

There are still bears out there. And wolves. And fish. And squirrels. Not as many as there were, but there still are a few. You see signs of them all, every now and again.

I don't think they're going to get everybody. These things with the tracks. I don't think they're going to get every single person on the planet. I think that if they were able to do that they would have done that already.

They might get most of us. But they won't get all of us.

You just gotta think about us, like people, like a forest, or a mine, or an oil field. When miners go into a mine, they mine that mine not until the mine's one hundred percent empty, you know what I mean? They might get close. They might get 99.9 percent of whatever mineral out of that mine, but they won't get all of it. They'll stop mining that mine the instant the thing starts costing more than it produces in revenue. You get me?

Like, the instant it starts getting cost ineffective to gather the last little bits of whatever resource, that's when a company gets up and moves on to another deposit, somewhere else, is what I'm talking about. If they had the ability to get all of us, they would have done it by now. The fact that there are people here and there, still, I mean, to me . . . that gives me a lot of hope, really.

Because the people who are left . . . I mean, think about it. Here in the park. Four people. That I know about. You, me, that Samantha lady, and the crazy racist fella. This park has an area of more than seventy-five hundred square kilometres.

I'm not saying they're gone. Don't get me wrong there. But I just think if they had the ability to get every single one of us, it would have happened by now.

So try and keep your head down and enjoy the aurora borealis when it comes out. Don't attract attention to yourself and maybe they'll get tired of looking for ya. And while you're at it, respect the other campers and don't start any fires you can't put out.

Oh, and try and leave any place you stay better than when you found it. That's a big one, too. That's the most important rule in life.

Wanna check out Opeongo Lake with me?

It's breathtaking.

LOWELL (OPEONGO LAKE, ON)

I've read all of the park pamphlets they got here. Read a book about the history of the lake. Opeongo. The name means "sandy at the narrows."

There are no waves here. I was supposed to be going to Tofino. Existence is pretty random, I think.

It started to get hot, so I took my shirt off. I'm lying here in the sun. Looking at this lake. *Opeongo.* Life gets sandy at the narrows. Life is a lake when you're chasing an ocean. It's a shallow lake. But I can see my reflection in its surface. I can see the scars on my face.

Half my eyesight left. A pretty noticeable limp. Two missing teeth.

But this has turned out to be a very durable tape recorder. The light doesn't come on anymore when I use it but the wheels still turn. It still records and everything. Good work, tape recorder. Good work, buddy.

There's kind of a buzzing of insects you can hear across the water. I don't know if they're cicadas or crickets or what. This kind of drone.

I think I've figured out how to survive the end of the world.

See, I can hope Zoe or Ollie are still kicking around, and then I can take Bird's Kawasaki and drive down to the gate there, but all of the hope in the world isn't going to affect whether or not I run into them.

But if I imagine that they're still there. Zoe in her office. Ollie in his cabin. That, at least, gives me something. Enough to keep going. That gives me all I need to carry on. I don't even have to go down there and check in on them. I'm good to stay here a while longer.

Maintain my low profile. If I can imagine they're still doing okay, that's all I need.

If I can imagine the purple lights are gonna go away soon, that's all I need. That'll get me through another day. It's imagination, not hope. That's the trick to surviving. Imagination gives you strength, gives you new ideas, changes things up.

Sometimes, you gotta put your ear up to the shell. Because some people only ever get one ocean.

Jane is safe. She's somewhere else, but she's safe. JP's safe. He's somewhere else, but he's . . . see, if I can imagine it . . . Connor, he's . . .

Maybe I'm losing it again. Maybe I am. If I'm losing it this time, though, I'm losing it in a different way. A good way. I'm not in a funk anymore. I've snapped out of it.

Because I heard wolves howling last night. Actual wolves. After the purple lights died down. Across the lake. Opeongo. Real-life wolves. According to the pamphlets, it's way out of season.

First time I ever heard real wolves howl. It's amazing. They sound like a commitment. All of them together. Howling for real. They sounded like how Jane and I felt. How she made me feel. In Montreal. Tremolo. Like there were two notes. Call and answer. Give and take.

How could you turn your back on noise like that? How could you ever?

I think I'm going to take one of the rental canoes and go find them. Them, across the lake.

I might not ever see another person again.

That's okay.

I got a fortune of wolves.

End of tape #F-498C45.

ACKNOWLEDGEMENTS

Special thanks to the Playwrights Atlantic Resource Centre, Arts NB, the Canada Council for the Arts, Thomas Morgan Jones, Jenny Munday, Falen Johnson, Natalie Sappier, Colleen Murphy, German Saravanja, Brandon Coffey, John Rairdon, Nick Grimson, Neil Young, and Joanna Bryson.

Ryan Griffith is a playwright from Woodstock, New Brunswick. A graduate of the National Theatre School of Canada, his play *Lutz* was published by Playwrights Canada Press in 2011. His short play, *Shepody, Rage and Wolfe*, was produced by Theatre Yes in Edmonton and Halifax, and his original plays *Returning Fire* and *Fortune of Wolves*, as well as his adaptation of Alistair MacLeod's *The Boat*, have been produced by Theatre New Brunswick in Fredericton. His newest play, *A Brief History of the Maritimes and Everywhere Else*, debuted with the company in March 2019.

First edition: November 2019
Printed and bound in Canada by Imprimerie Gauvin, Gatineau

Jacket art and design by Geordan Moore / The Quarrelsome Yeti
Press, https://yetifight.com/
Author photo © Lorne Power

**PLAYWRIGHTS
CANADA PRESS**
202-269 Richmond St. W.
Toronto, ON
M5V 1X1

416.703.0013
info@playwrightscanada.com
www.playwrightscanada.com
@playcanpress